Other books in the Strangers In Paradise series

VOLUME ONE

The Collected Strangers In Paradise

VOLUME TWO

I Dream Of You

It's A Good Life

VOLUME THREE

Love Me Tender

Immortal Enemies

High School

Sanctuary

My Other Life

Child Of Rage

Tropic Of Desire

Brave New World

Heart In Hand

Flower To Flame

DAVID'S STORY

DAVID'S STORY

TERRY MOORE

ABSTRACT STUDIO
HOUSTON, TEXAS

TERRY MOORE
Story and Art

ROBYN MOORE
Publisher

BRIAN MILLER
Color

GUSTAVE DORE
Biblical Illustrations

Strangers In Paradise: DAVID'S STORY
Copyright ©2004 Terry Moore
All Rights Reserved

First Edition: June 2004
ISBN 1-892597-25-X

Published by
Abstract Studio, Inc.
P. O. Box 271487
Houston, Texas 77277
www.StrangersInParadise.com
email: SIPNET@StrangersInParadise.com

Printed In Canada

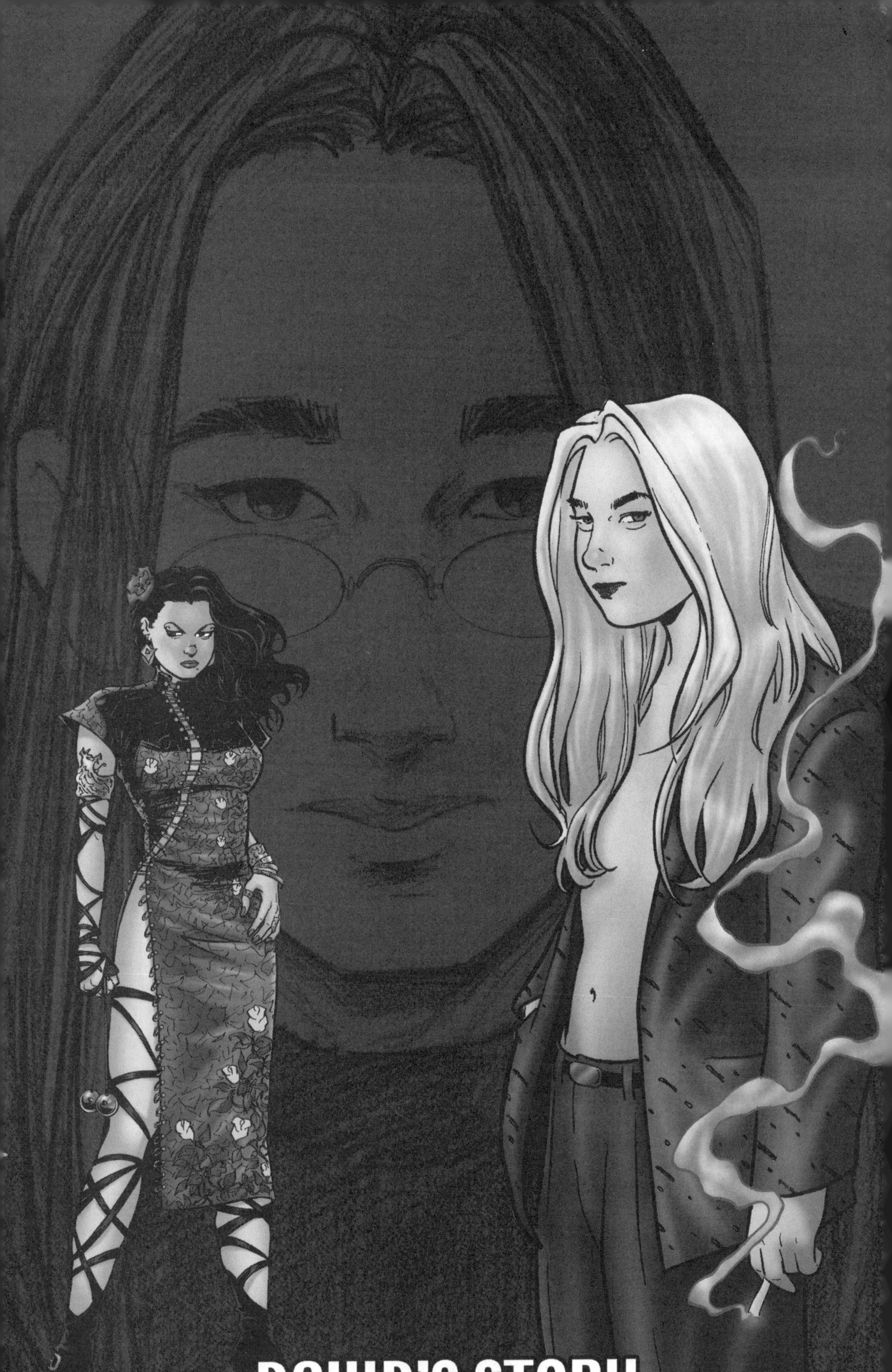

DAVID'S STORY

No one is righteous, no, not one;
  no one understands;
  no one seeks for God.
All have turned aside;
  together they have become worthless;
  no one does good, not even one.
Their throat is an open grave;
  they use their tongues to deceive.
The venom of asps is under their lips.
Their mouth is full of curses and bitterness.
Their feet are swift to shed blood;
  in their paths are ruin and misery,
  and the way of peace they have not known.
There is no fear of God before their eyes.

—St. Paul

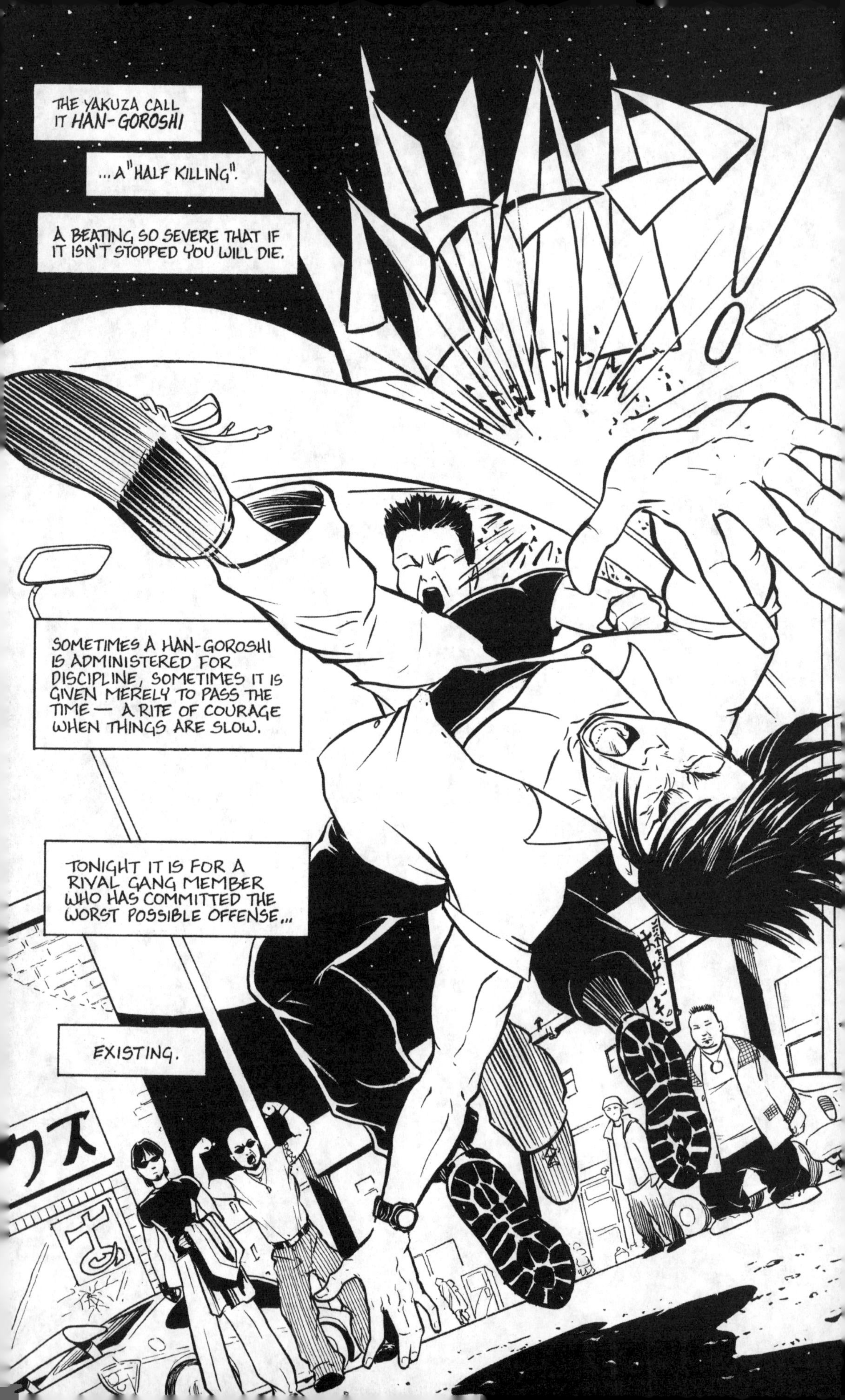
THE YAKUZA CALL IT HAN-GOROSHI
...A "HALF KILLING".
A BEATING SO SEVERE THAT IF IT ISN'T STOPPED YOU WILL DIE.
SOMETIMES A HAN-GOROSHI IS ADMINISTERED FOR DISCIPLINE, SOMETIMES IT IS GIVEN MERELY TO PASS THE TIME— A RITE OF COURAGE WHEN THINGS ARE SLOW.
TONIGHT IT IS FOR A RIVAL GANG MEMBER WHO HAS COMMITTED THE WORST POSSIBLE OFFENSE...
EXISTING.

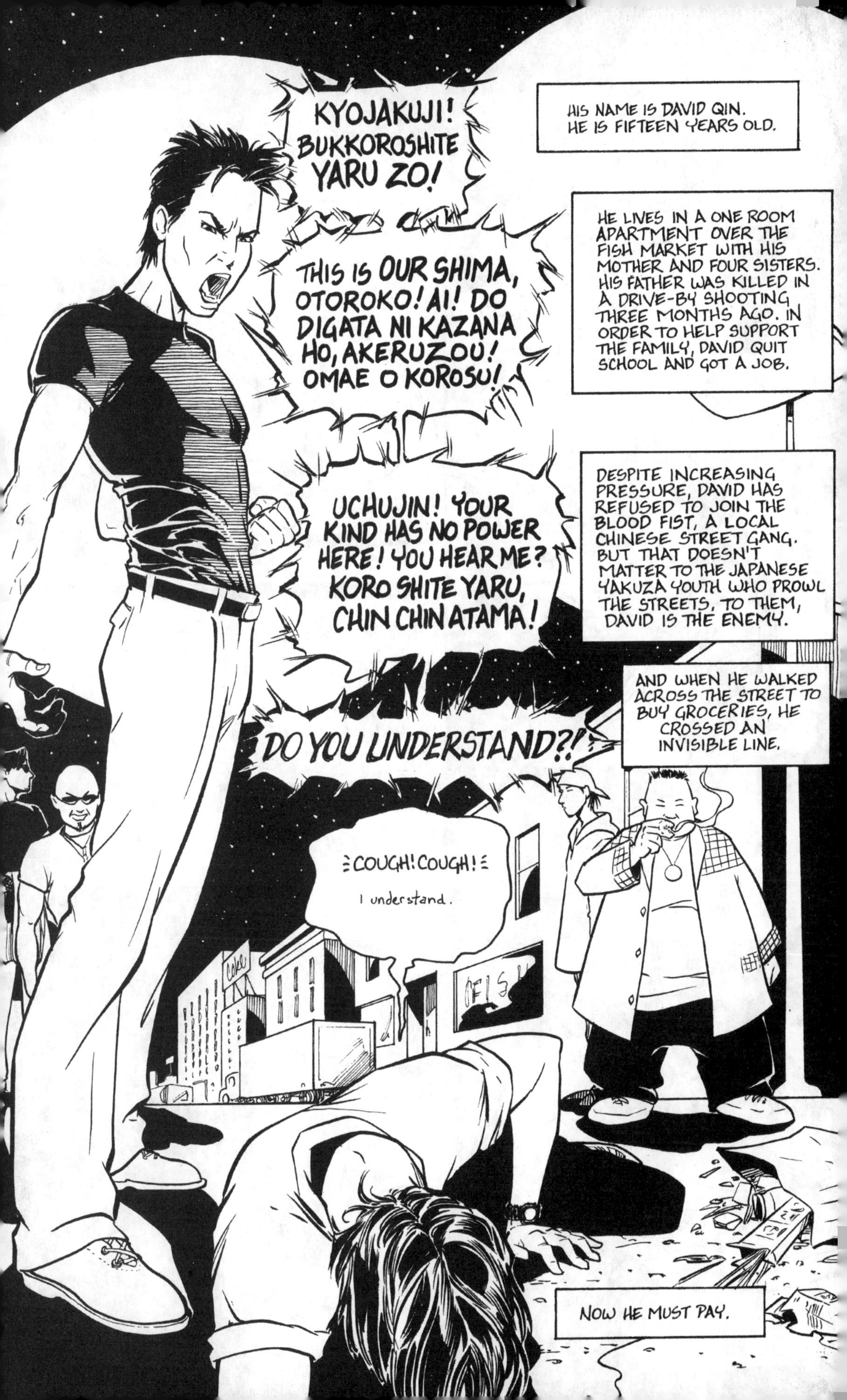
HIS NAME IS DAVID QIN.
HE IS FIFTEEN YEARS OLD.
KYOJAKUJI! BUKKOROSHITE YARU ZO!
HE LIVES IN A ONE ROOM APARTMENT OVER THE FISH MARKET WITH HIS MOTHER AND FOUR SISTERS. HIS FATHER WAS KILLED IN A DRIVE-BY SHOOTING THREE MONTHS AGO. IN ORDER TO HELP SUPPORT THE FAMILY, DAVID QUIT SCHOOL AND GOT A JOB.
THIS IS OUR SHIMA, OTOROKO! AI! DO DIGATA NI KAZANA HO, AKERUZOU! OMAE O KOROSU!
DESPITE INCREASING PRESSURE, DAVID HAS REFUSED TO JOIN THE BLOOD FIST, A LOCAL CHINESE STREET GANG. BUT THAT DOESN'T MATTER TO THE JAPANESE YAKUZA YOUTH WHO PROWL THE STREETS. TO THEM, DAVID IS THE ENEMY.
UCHUJIN! YOUR KIND HAS NO POWER HERE! YOU HEAR ME? KORO SHITE YARU, CHIN CHIN ATAMA!
AND WHEN HE WALKED ACROSS THE STREET TO BUY GROCERIES, HE CROSSED AN INVISIBLE LINE.
DO YOU UNDERSTAND?!
COUGH! COUGH!
I understand.
NOW HE MUST PAY.

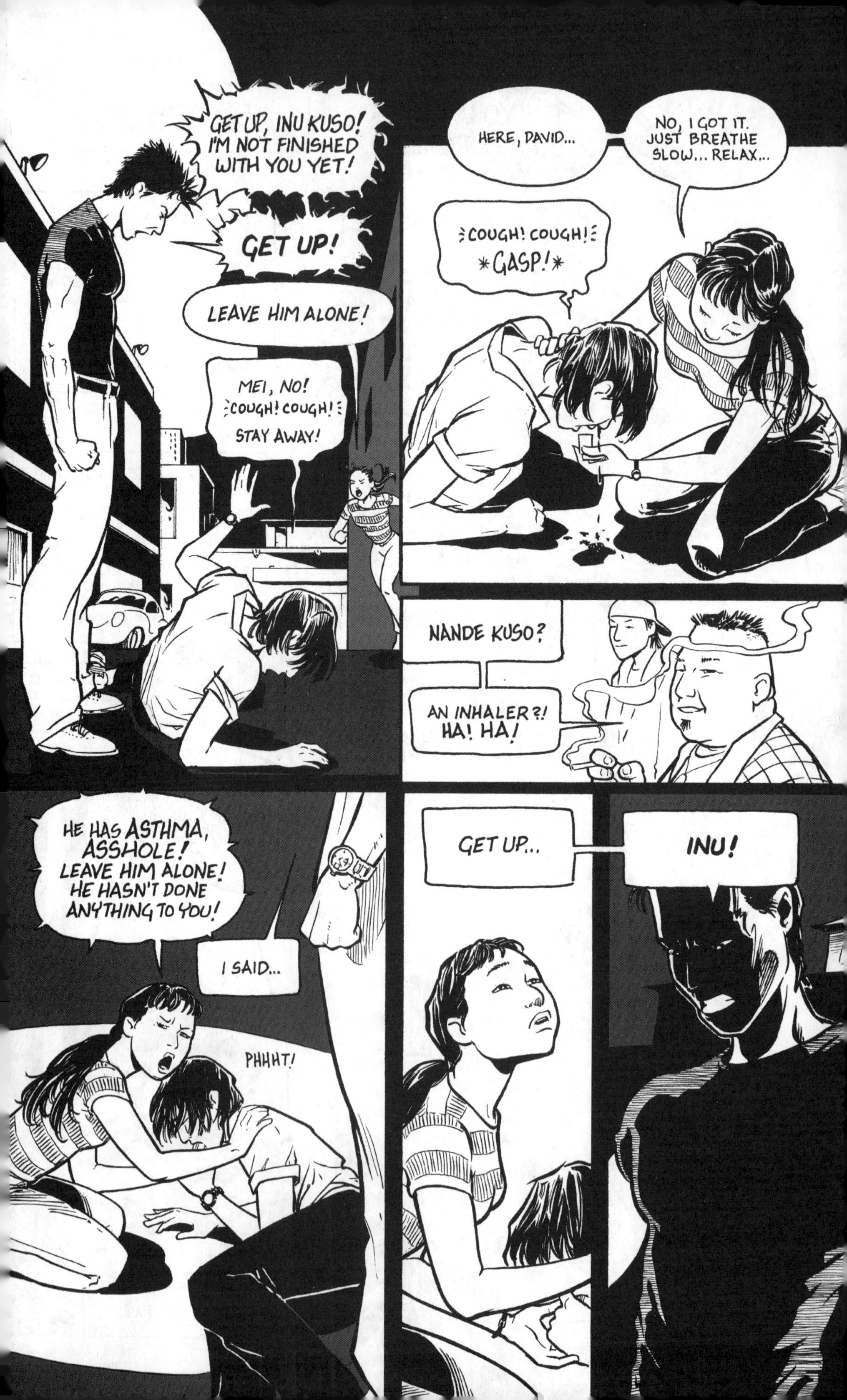
GET UP, INU KUSO! I'M NOT FINISHED WITH YOU YET!
GET UP!
LEAVE HIM ALONE!
MEI, NO! COUGH! COUGH! STAY AWAY!
HERE, DAVID...
NO, I GOT IT. JUST BREATHE SLOW... RELAX...
COUGH! COUGH! *GASP!*
NANDE KUSO?
AN INHALER?! HA! HA!
HE HAS ASTHMA, ASSHOLE! LEAVE HIM ALONE! HE HASN'T DONE ANYTHING TO YOU!
I SAID...
PHHHT!
GET UP...
INU!

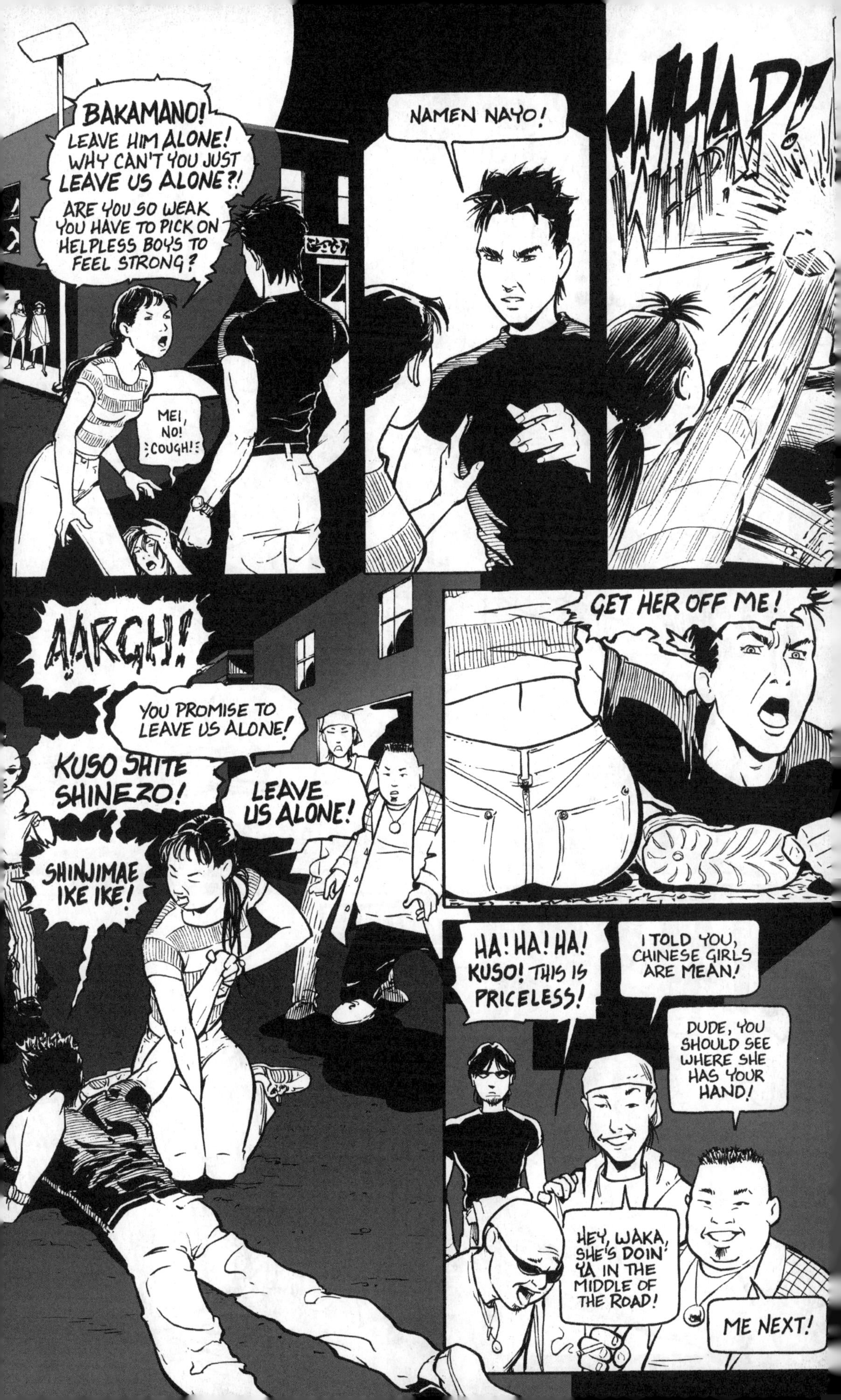
BAKAMANO!
LEAVE HIM ALONE! WHY CAN'T YOU JUST LEAVE US ALONE?! ARE YOU SO WEAK YOU HAVE TO PICK ON HELPLESS BOYS TO FEEL STRONG?
MEI, NO! ;COUGH!;
NAMEN NAYO!
WHAP!
WHAP!!
AARGH!
YOU PROMISE TO LEAVE US ALONE!
KUSO SHITE SHINEZO!
LEAVE US ALONE!
SHINJIMAE IKE IKE!
GET HER OFF ME!
HA! HA! HA! KUSO! THIS IS PRICELESS!
I TOLD YOU, CHINESE GIRLS ARE MEAN!
DUDE, YOU SHOULD SEE WHERE SHE HAS YOUR HAND!
HEY, WAKA, SHE'S DOIN' YA IN THE MIDDLE OF THE ROAD!
ME NEXT!

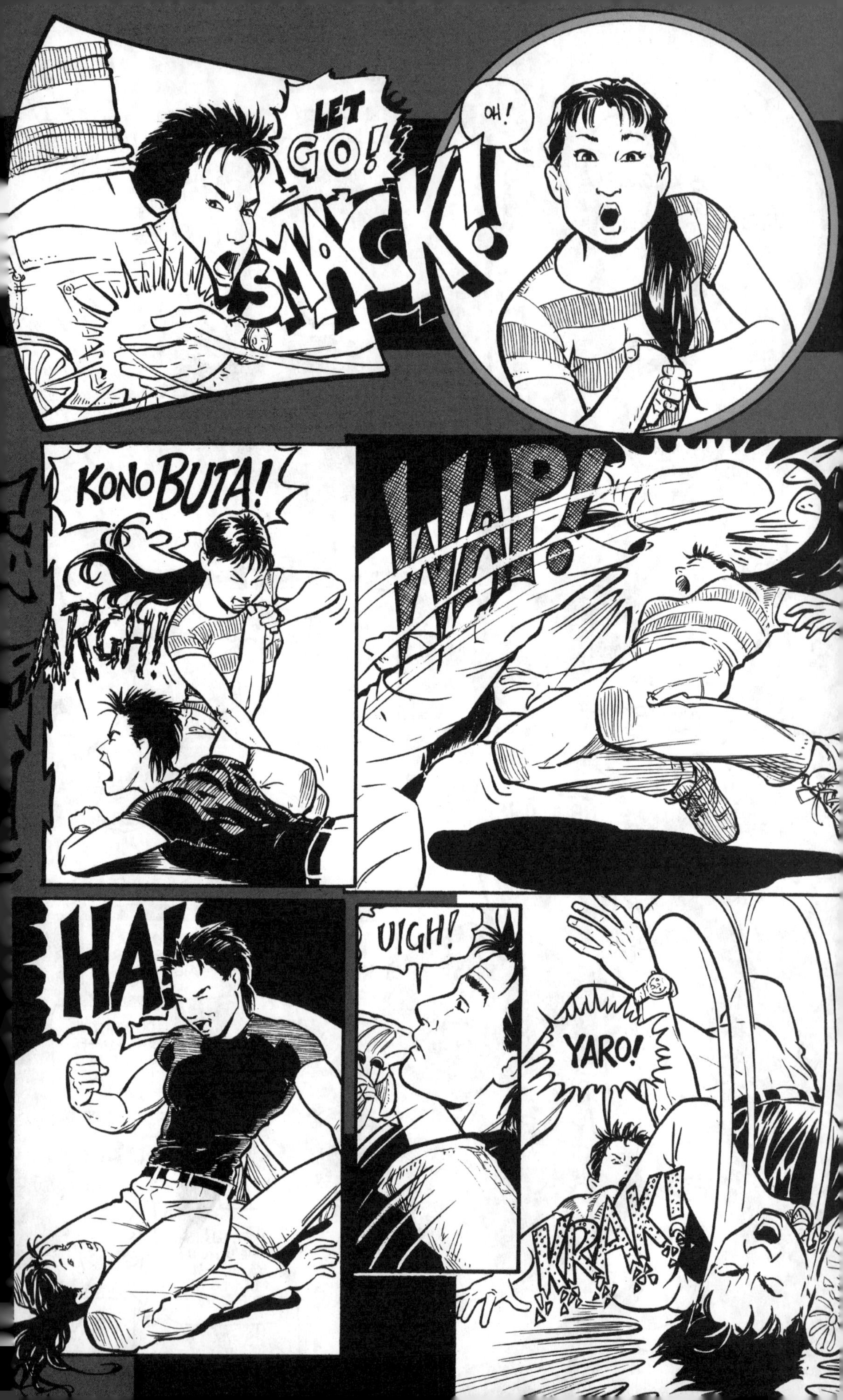

LET GO!
SMACK!
OH!
KONO BUTA!
ARGH!
WAP!
HA!
UIGH!
YARO!
KRAK!

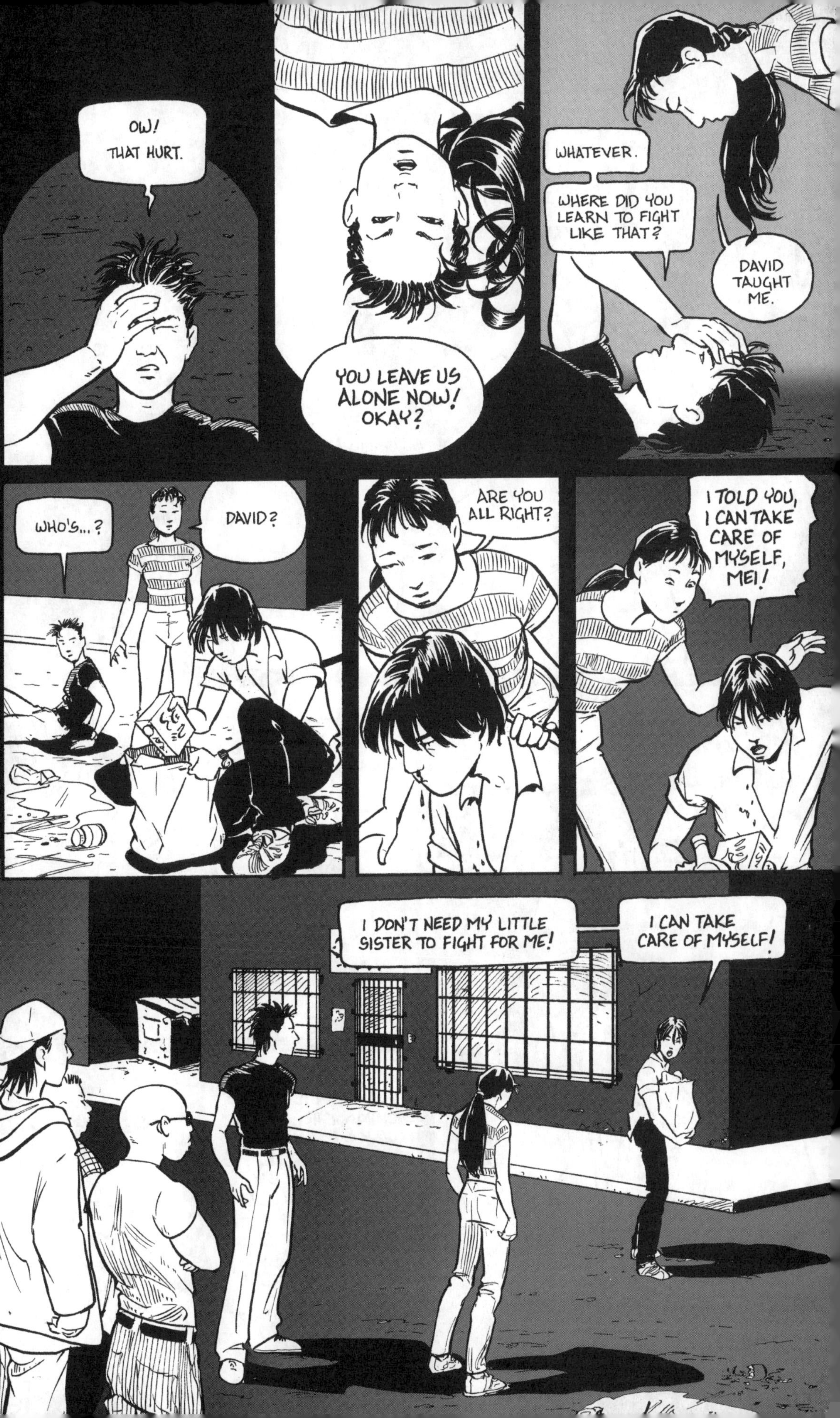
OW!
THAT HURT.
YOU LEAVE US ALONE NOW! OKAY?
WHATEVER.
WHERE DID YOU LEARN TO FIGHT LIKE THAT?
DAVID TAUGHT ME.
WHO'S...?
DAVID?
ARE YOU ALL RIGHT?
I TOLD YOU, I CAN TAKE CARE OF MYSELF, MEI!
I DON'T NEED MY LITTLE SISTER TO FIGHT FOR ME!
I CAN TAKE CARE OF MYSELF!

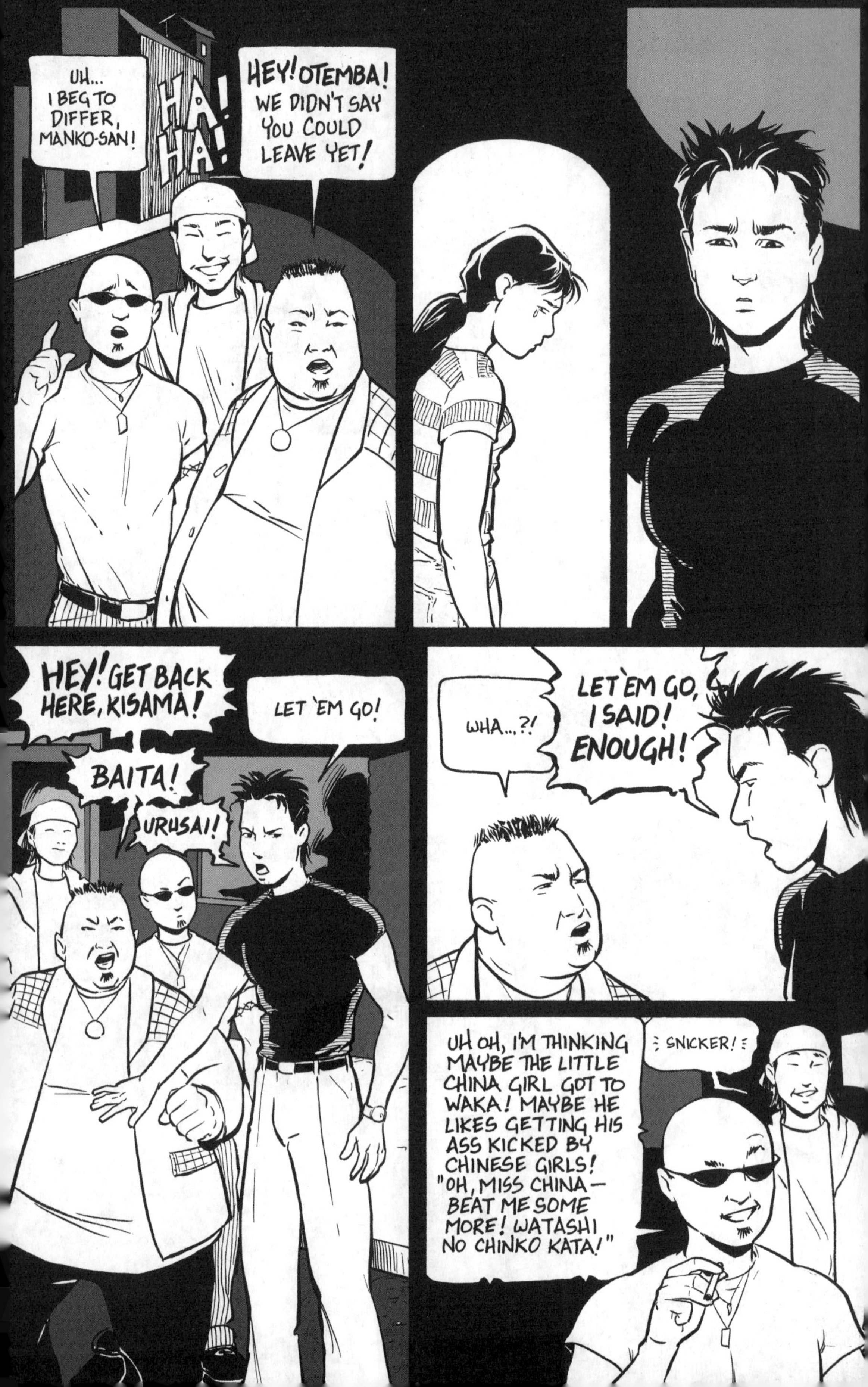
UH... I BEG TO DIFFER, MANKO-SAN!
HA! HA! HA!
HEY! OTEMBA! WE DIDN'T SAY YOU COULD LEAVE YET!
HEY! GET BACK HERE, KISAMA!
LET 'EM GO!
BAITA!
URUSAI!
WHA...?!
LET 'EM GO, I SAID! ENOUGH!
UH OH, I'M THINKING MAYBE THE LITTLE CHINA GIRL GOT TO WAKA! MAYBE HE LIKES GETTING HIS ASS KICKED BY CHINESE GIRLS! "OH, MISS CHINA— BEAT ME SOME MORE! WATASHI NO CHINKO KATA!"
SNICKER!

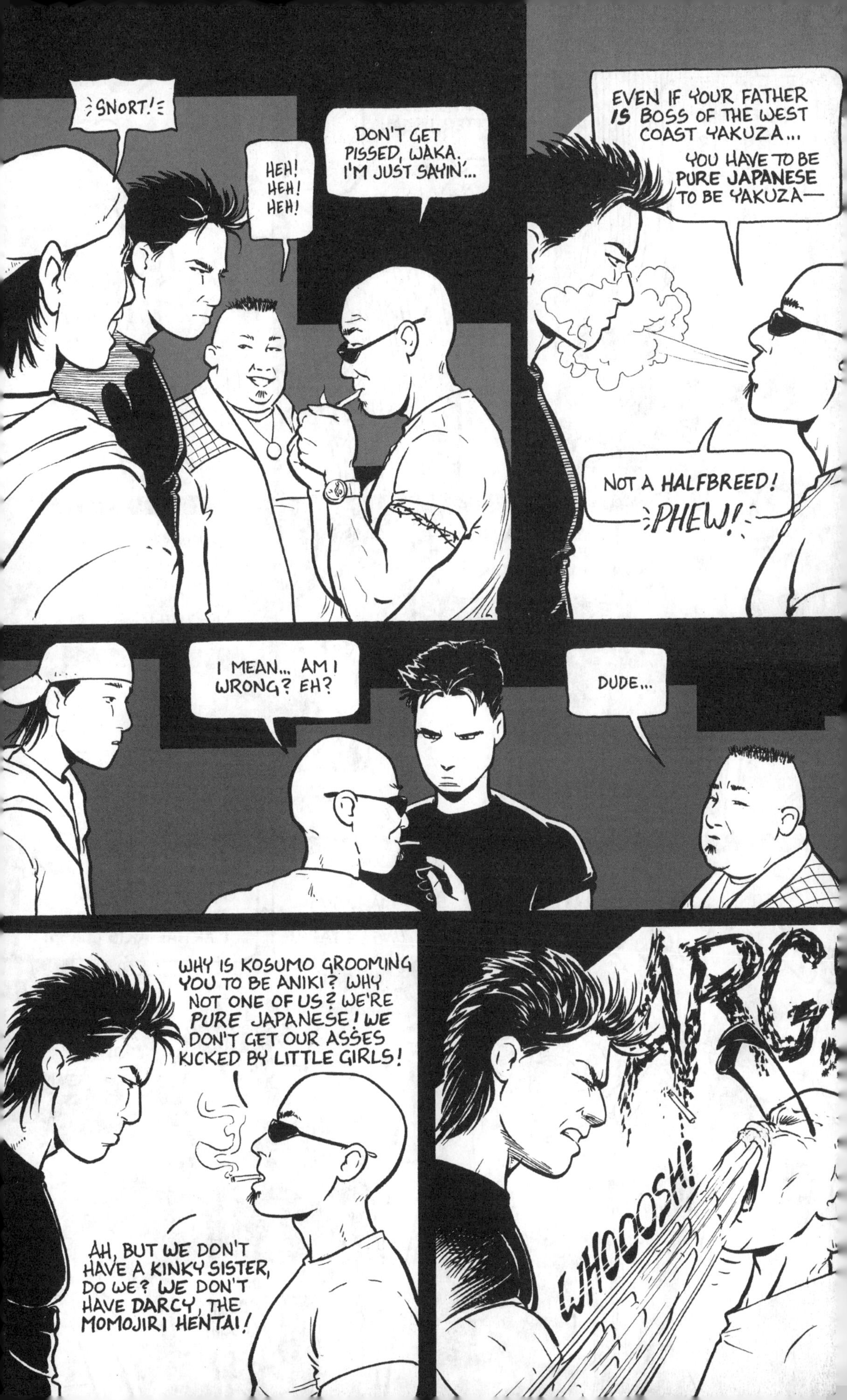
SNORT!
HEH! HEH! HEH!
DON'T GET PISSED, WAKA. I'M JUST SAYIN'...
EVEN IF YOUR FATHER IS BOSS OF THE WEST COAST YAKUZA...
YOU HAVE TO BE PURE JAPANESE TO BE YAKUZA—
NOT A HALFBREED!
PHEW!
I MEAN... AM I WRONG? EH?
DUDE...
WHY IS KOSUMO GROOMING YOU TO BE ANIKI? WHY NOT ONE OF US? WE'RE PURE JAPANESE! WE DON'T GET OUR ASSES KICKED BY LITTLE GIRLS!
AH, BUT WE DON'T HAVE A KINKY SISTER, DO WE? WE DON'T HAVE DARCY, THE MOMOJIRI HENTAI!
WHOOOOSH!

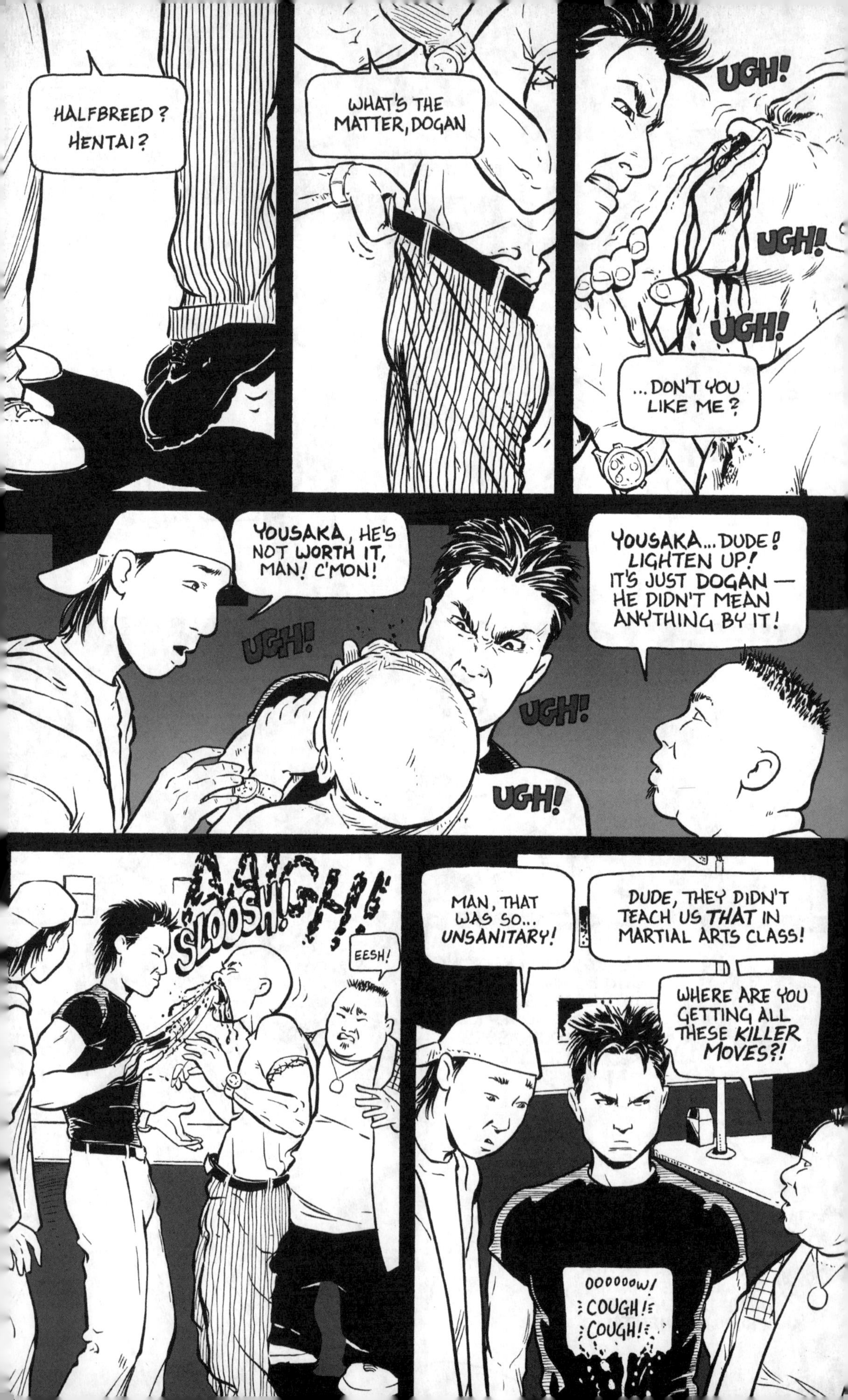
HALFBREED? HENTAI?
WHAT'S THE MATTER, DOGAN
UGH!
UGH!
UGH!
...DON'T YOU LIKE ME?
YOUSAKA, HE'S NOT WORTH IT, MAN! C'MON!
YOUSAKA... DUDE! LIGHTEN UP! IT'S JUST DOGAN — HE DIDN'T MEAN ANYTHING BY IT!
UGH!
UGH!
UGH!
SLOOSH!
EESH!
MAN, THAT WAS SO... UNSANITARY!
DUDE, THEY DIDN'T TEACH US THAT IN MARTIAL ARTS CLASS!
WHERE ARE YOU GETTING ALL THESE KILLER MOVES?!
OOOOOOW!
COUGH!
COUGH!

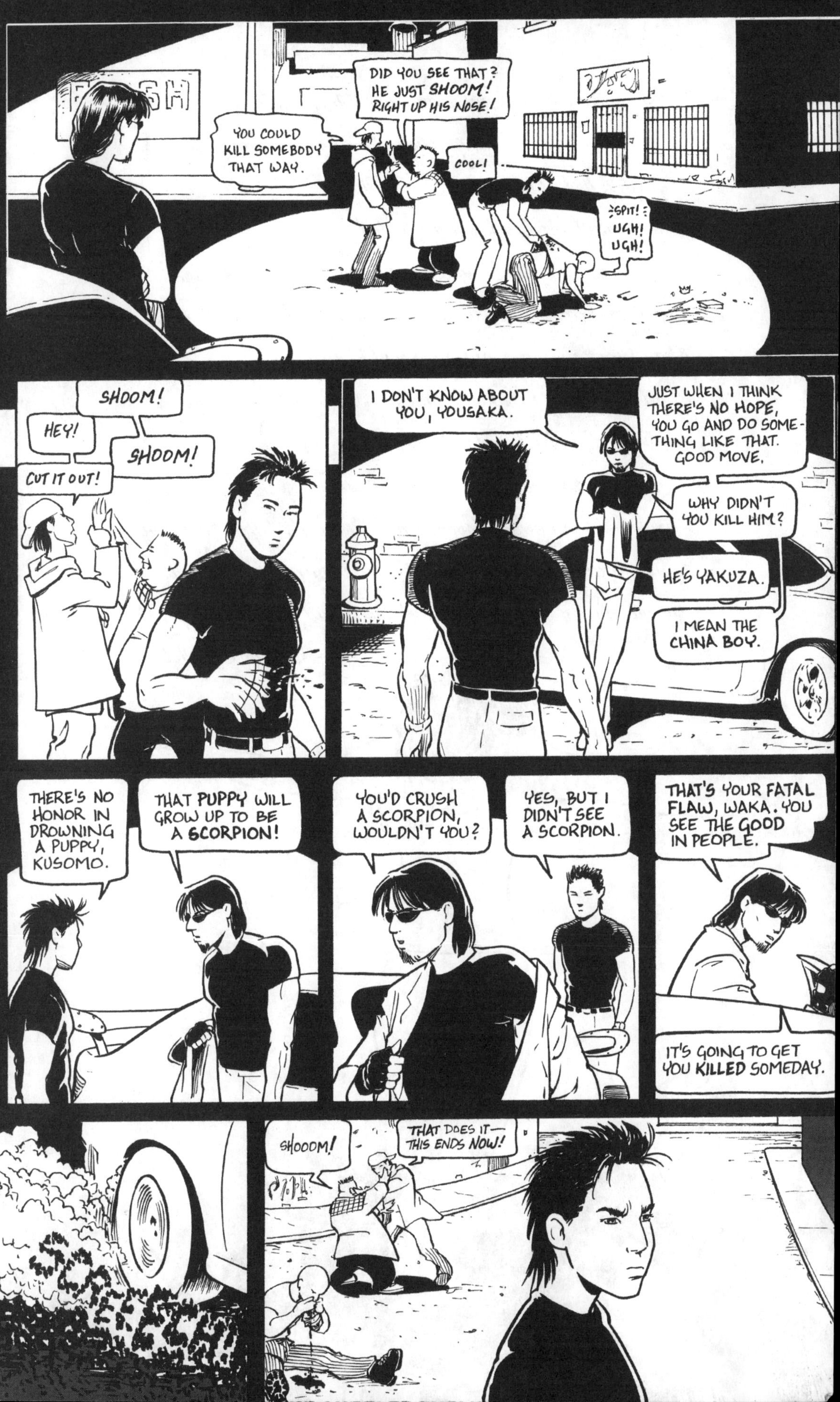

YOU COULD KILL SOMEBODY THAT WAY.
DID YOU SEE THAT? HE JUST SHOOM! RIGHT UP HIS NOSE!
COOL!
SPIT! UGH! UGH!
SHOOM!
HEY!
SHOOM!
CUT IT OUT!
I DON'T KNOW ABOUT YOU, YOUSAKA.
JUST WHEN I THINK THERE'S NO HOPE, YOU GO AND DO SOMETHING LIKE THAT. GOOD MOVE.
WHY DIDN'T YOU KILL HIM?
HE'S YAKUZA.
I MEAN THE CHINA BOY.
THERE'S NO HONOR IN DROWNING A PUPPY, KUSOMO.
THAT PUPPY WILL GROW UP TO BE A SCORPION!
YOU'D CRUSH A SCORPION, WOULDN'T YOU?
YES, BUT I DIDN'T SEE A SCORPION.
THAT'S YOUR FATAL FLAW, WAKA. YOU SEE THE GOOD IN PEOPLE.
IT'S GOING TO GET YOU KILLED SOMEDAY.
SHOOOM!
THAT DOES IT— THIS ENDS NOW!

"You have captivated my heart, my sister, my bride,
you have captivated my heart with one glance of your eyes.
A garden locked is my sister, my bride,
a spring locked, a fountain sealed.
Open to me, my sister, my love, my dove, my perfect one,
for my head is wet with dew, my locks with the drops of the night."
I had put off my garment; how could I put it on?
I had bathed my feet; how could I soil them?
My beloved put his hand to the latch,
and my heart was thrilled within me.
I arose to open to my beloved, and my hands dripped with myrrh,
my fingers with liquid myrrh, on the handles of the bolt.
I opened to my beloved, but my beloved had turned and gone.

~Song Of Solomon

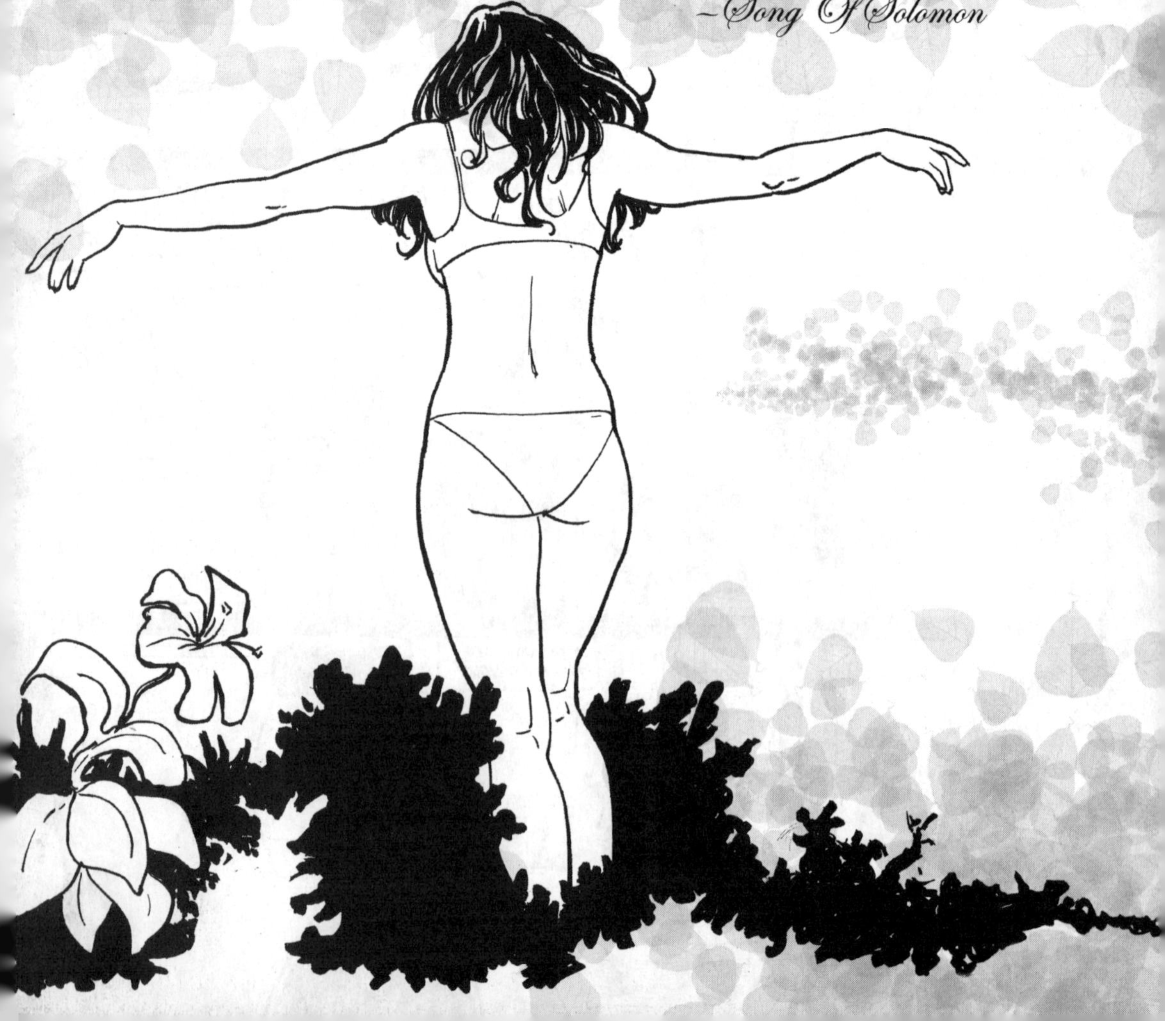

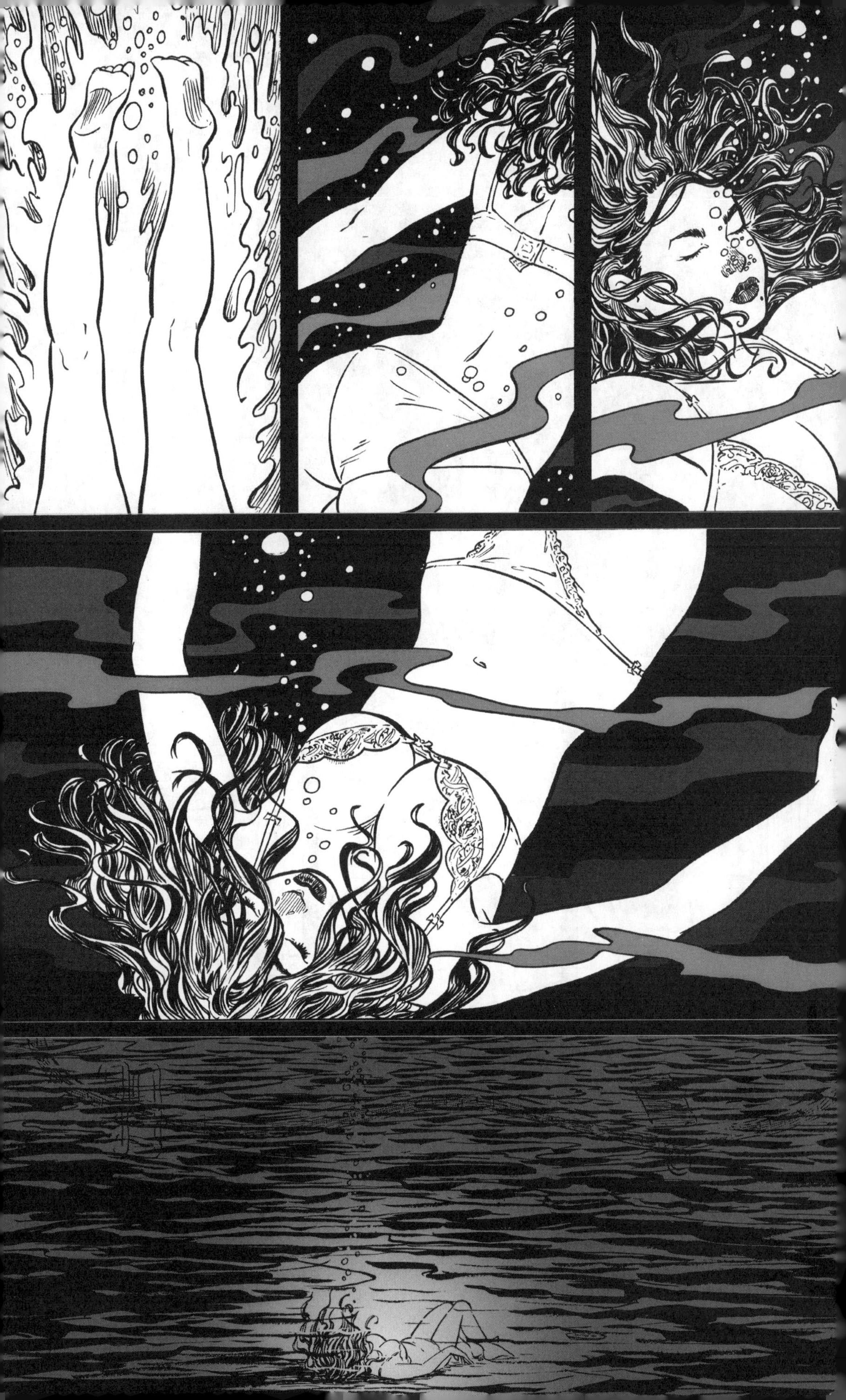

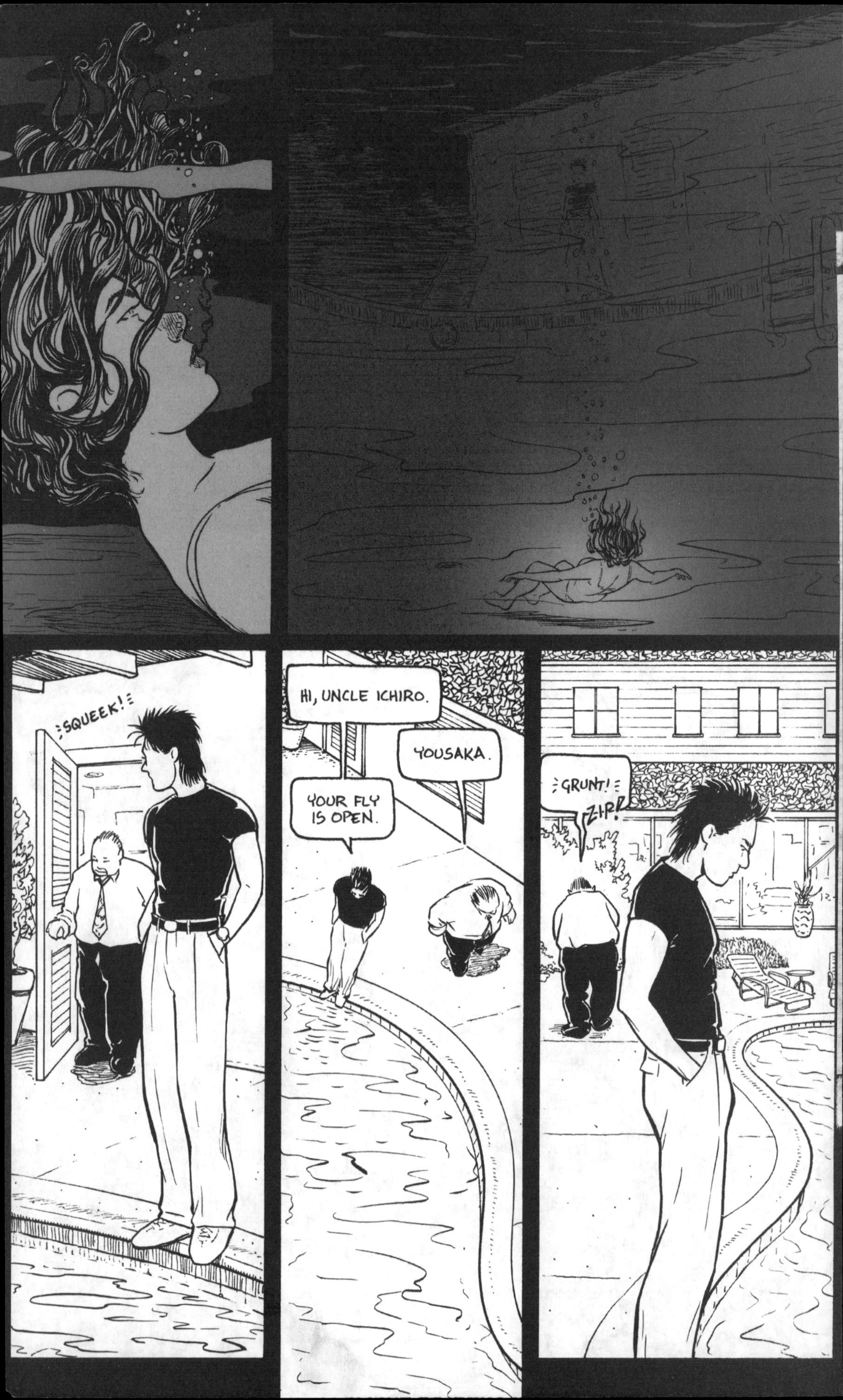
SQUEEK!
HI, UNCLE ICHIRO.
YOUR FLY IS OPEN.
YOUSAKA.
GRUNT!
ZIP!

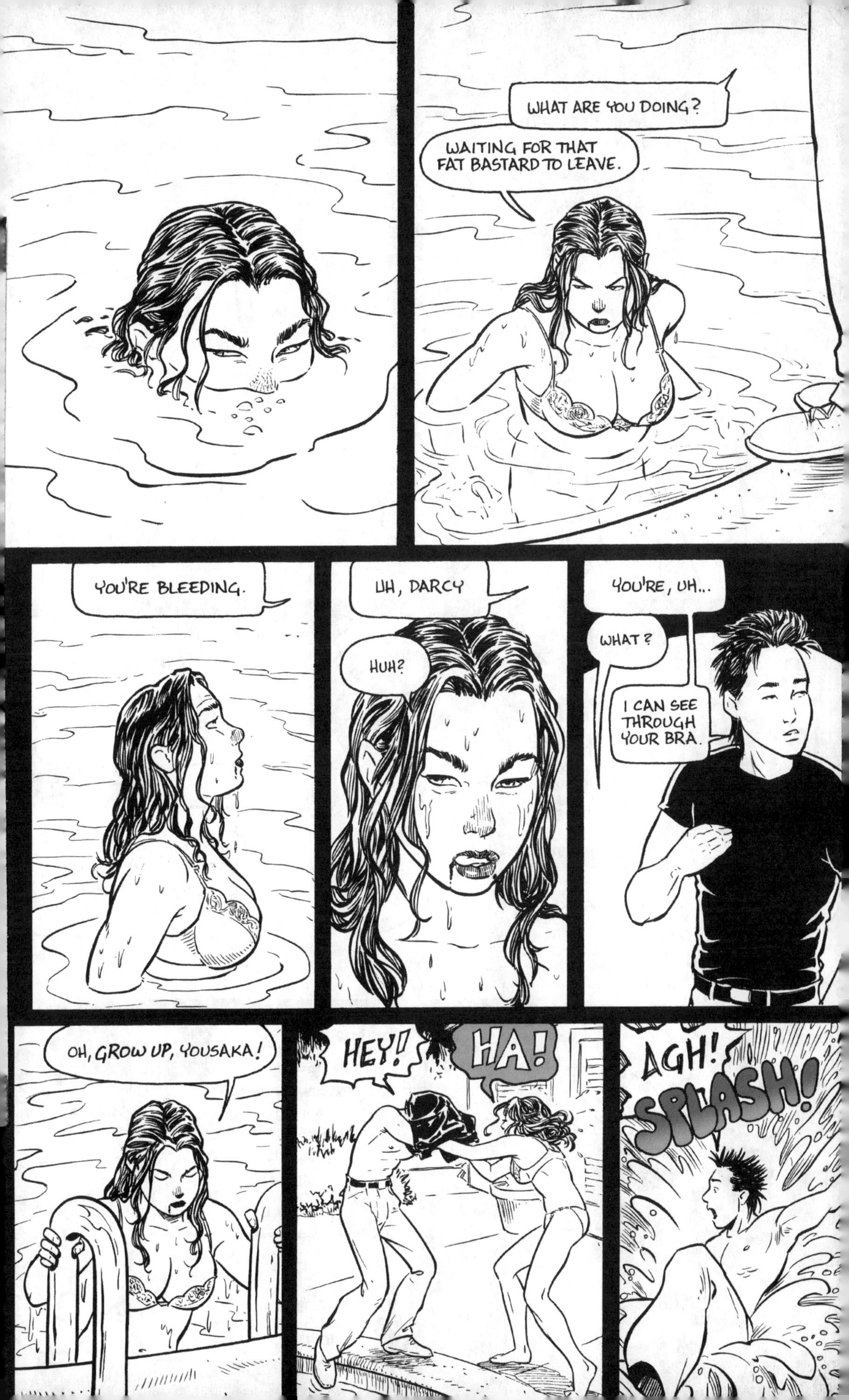
WHAT ARE YOU DOING?
WAITING FOR THAT FAT BASTARD TO LEAVE.
YOU'RE BLEEDING.
UH, DARCY
HUH?
YOU'RE, UH...
WHAT?
I CAN SEE THROUGH YOUR BRA.
OH, GROW UP, YOUSAKA!
HEY!
HA!
AGH!
SPLASH!

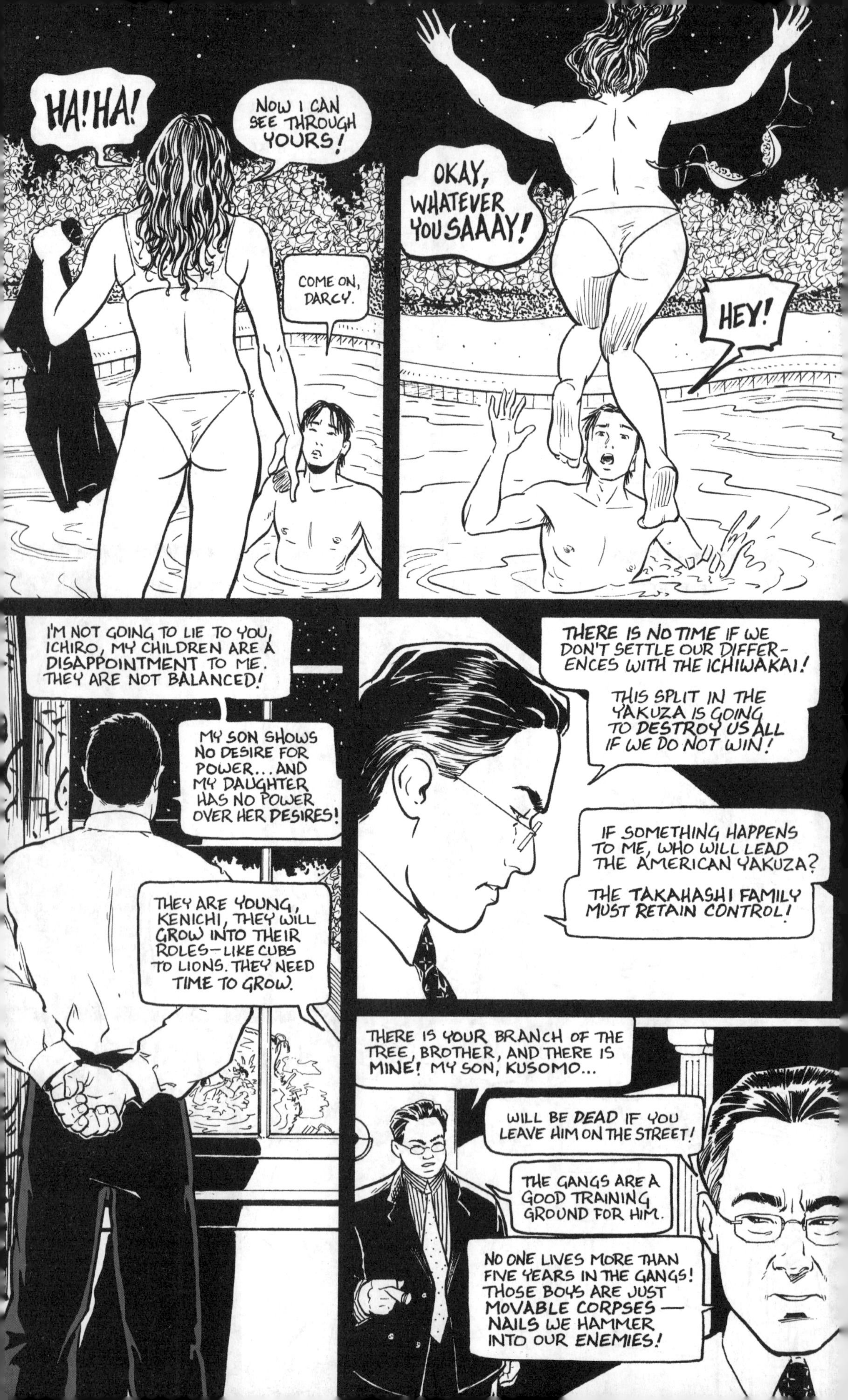
HA! HA!
NOW I CAN SEE THROUGH YOURS!
COME ON, DARCY.
OKAY, WHATEVER YOU SAAAY!
HEY!
I'M NOT GOING TO LIE TO YOU, ICHIRO, MY CHILDREN ARE A DISAPPOINTMENT TO ME. THEY ARE NOT BALANCED!
MY SON SHOWS NO DESIRE FOR POWER... AND MY DAUGHTER HAS NO POWER OVER HER DESIRES!
THEY ARE YOUNG, KENICHI, THEY WILL GROW INTO THEIR ROLES—LIKE CUBS TO LIONS. THEY NEED TIME TO GROW.
THERE IS NO TIME IF WE DON'T SETTLE OUR DIFFERENCES WITH THE ICHIWAKAI!
THIS SPLIT IN THE YAKUZA IS GOING TO DESTROY US ALL IF WE DO NOT WIN!
IF SOMETHING HAPPENS TO ME, WHO WILL LEAD THE AMERICAN YAKUZA?
THE TAKAHASHI FAMILY MUST RETAIN CONTROL!
THERE IS YOUR BRANCH OF THE TREE, BROTHER, AND THERE IS MINE! MY SON, KUSOMO...
WILL BE DEAD IF YOU LEAVE HIM ON THE STREET!
THE GANGS ARE A GOOD TRAINING GROUND FOR HIM.
NO ONE LIVES MORE THAN FIVE YEARS IN THE GANGS! THOSE BOYS ARE JUST MOVABLE CORPSES—NAILS WE HAMMER INTO OUR ENEMIES!

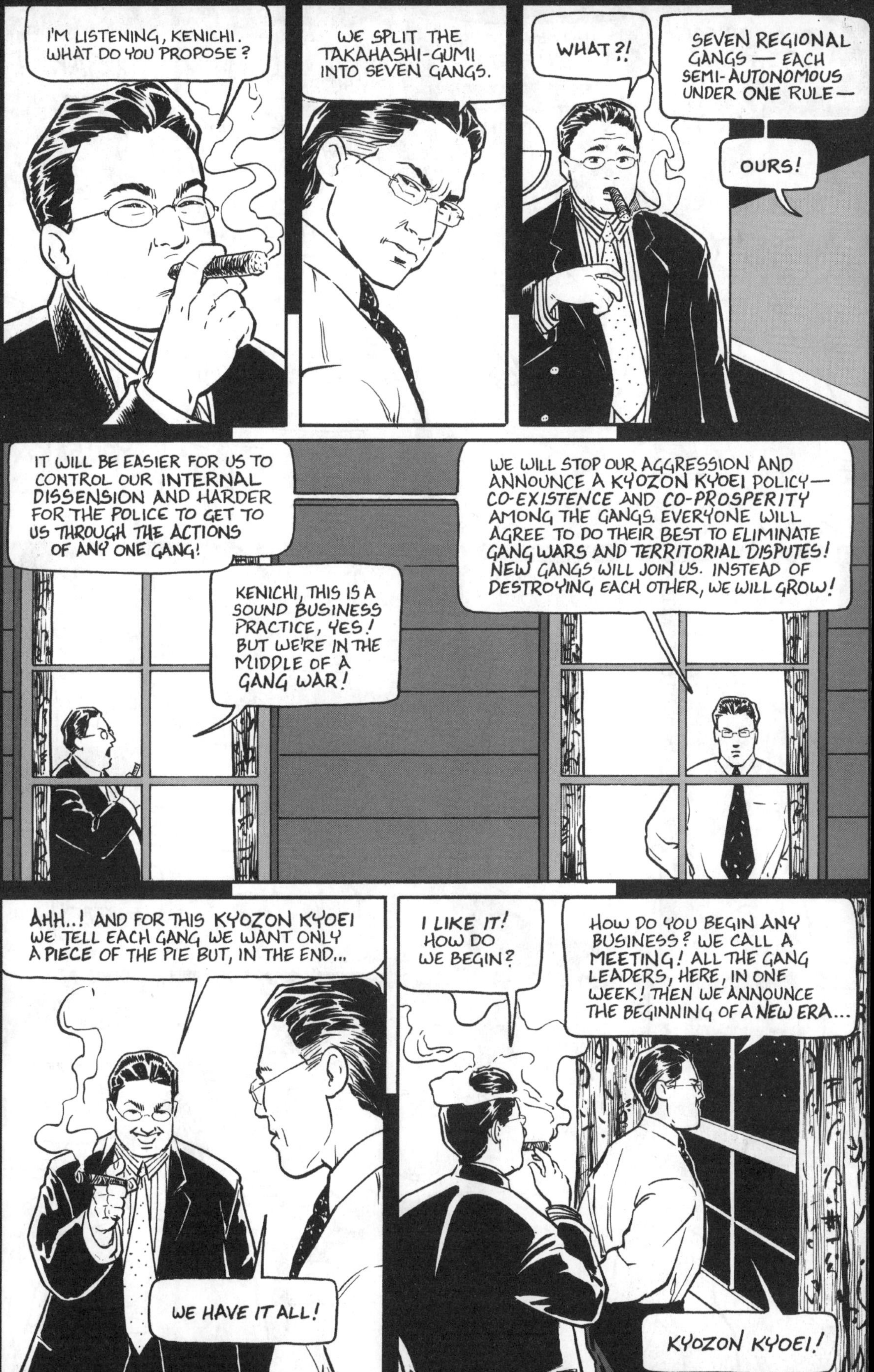
I'M LISTENING, KENICHI. WHAT DO YOU PROPOSE?
WE SPLIT THE TAKAHASHI-GUMI INTO SEVEN GANGS.
WHAT?!
SEVEN REGIONAL GANGS — EACH SEMI-AUTONOMOUS UNDER ONE RULE—
OURS!
IT WILL BE EASIER FOR US TO CONTROL OUR INTERNAL DISSENSION AND HARDER FOR THE POLICE TO GET TO US THROUGH THE ACTIONS OF ANY ONE GANG!
KENICHI, THIS IS A SOUND BUSINESS PRACTICE, YES! BUT WE'RE IN THE MIDDLE OF A GANG WAR!
WE WILL STOP OUR AGGRESSION AND ANNOUNCE A KYOZON KYOEI POLICY— CO-EXISTENCE AND CO-PROSPERITY AMONG THE GANGS. EVERYONE WILL AGREE TO DO THEIR BEST TO ELIMINATE GANG WARS AND TERRITORIAL DISPUTES! NEW GANGS WILL JOIN US. INSTEAD OF DESTROYING EACH OTHER, WE WILL GROW!
AHH..! AND FOR THIS KYOZON KYOEI WE TELL EACH GANG WE WANT ONLY A PIECE OF THE PIE BUT, IN THE END...
WE HAVE IT ALL!
I LIKE IT! HOW DO WE BEGIN?
HOW DO YOU BEGIN ANY BUSINESS? WE CALL A MEETING! ALL THE GANG LEADERS, HERE, IN ONE WEEK! THEN WE ANNOUNCE THE BEGINNING OF A NEW ERA...
KYOZON KYOEI!

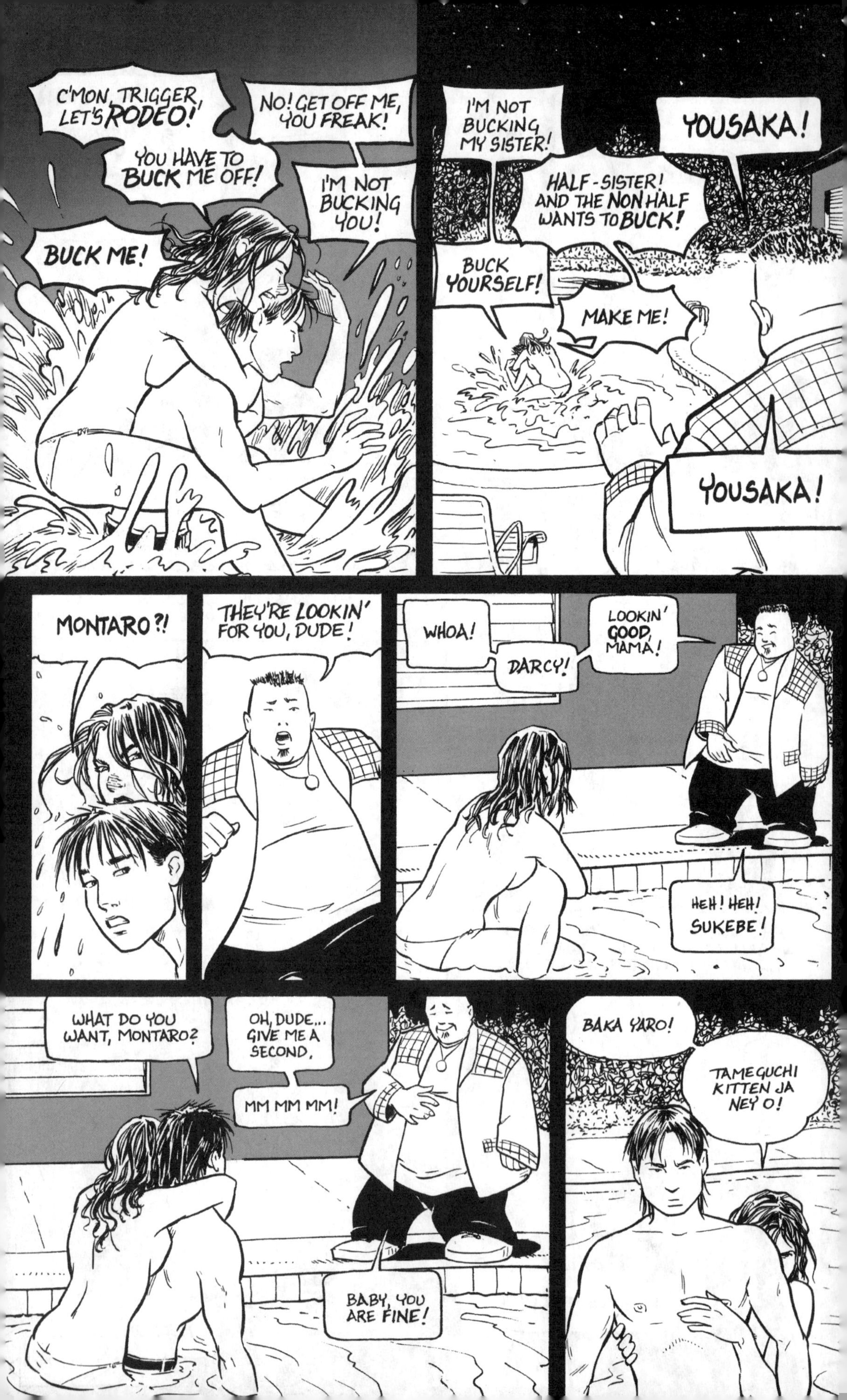

C'MON, TRIGGER, LET'S RODEO!
NO! GET OFF ME, YOU FREAK!
YOU HAVE TO BUCK ME OFF!
I'M NOT BUCKING YOU!
BUCK ME!
I'M NOT BUCKING MY SISTER!
YOUSAKA!
HALF-SISTER! AND THE NON HALF WANTS TO BUCK!
BUCK YOURSELF!
MAKE ME!
YOUSAKA!
MONTARO?!
THEY'RE LOOKIN' FOR YOU, DUDE!
WHOA!
DARCY!
LOOKIN' GOOD, MAMA!
HEH! HEH! SUKEBE!
WHAT DO YOU WANT, MONTARO?
OH, DUDE... GIVE ME A SECOND.
MM MM MM!
BABY, YOU ARE FINE!
BAKA YARO!
TAMEGUCHI KITTEN JA NEY O!

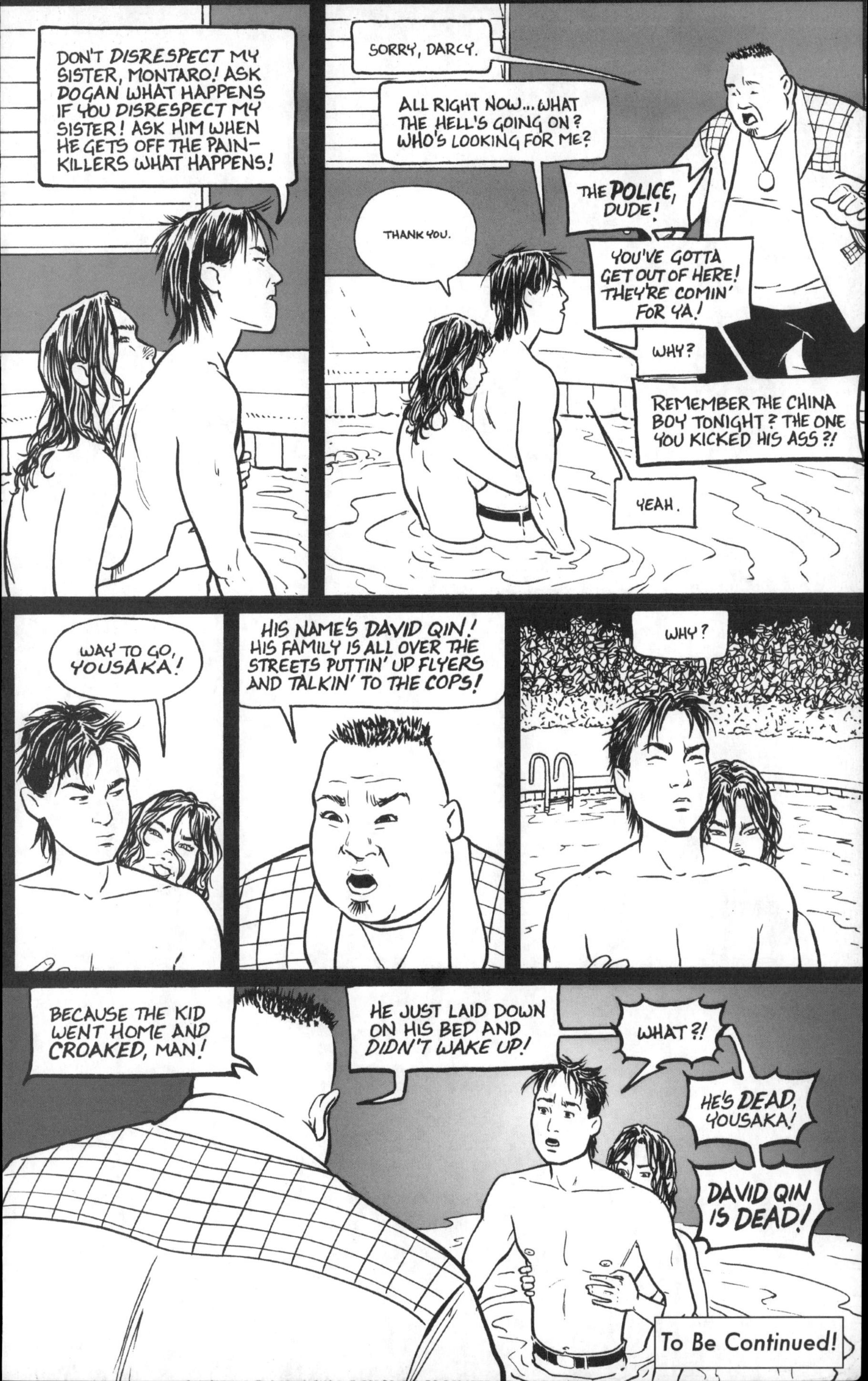

DON'T DISRESPECT MY SISTER, MONTARO! ASK DOGAN WHAT HAPPENS IF YOU DISRESPECT MY SISTER! ASK HIM WHEN HE GETS OFF THE PAIN-KILLERS WHAT HAPPENS!
SORRY, DARCY.
ALL RIGHT NOW... WHAT THE HELL'S GOING ON? WHO'S LOOKING FOR ME?
THANK YOU.
THE POLICE, DUDE!
YOU'VE GOTTA GET OUT OF HERE! THEY'RE COMIN' FOR YA!
WHY?
REMEMBER THE CHINA BOY TONIGHT? THE ONE YOU KICKED HIS ASS?!
YEAH.
WAY TO GO, YOUSAKA!
HIS NAME'S DAVID QIN! HIS FAMILY IS ALL OVER THE STREETS PUTTIN' UP FLYERS AND TALKIN' TO THE COPS!
WHY?
BECAUSE THE KID WENT HOME AND CROAKED, MAN!
HE JUST LAID DOWN ON HIS BED AND DIDN'T WAKE UP!
WHAT?!
HE'S DEAD, YOUSAKA!
DAVID QIN IS DEAD!
To Be Continued!

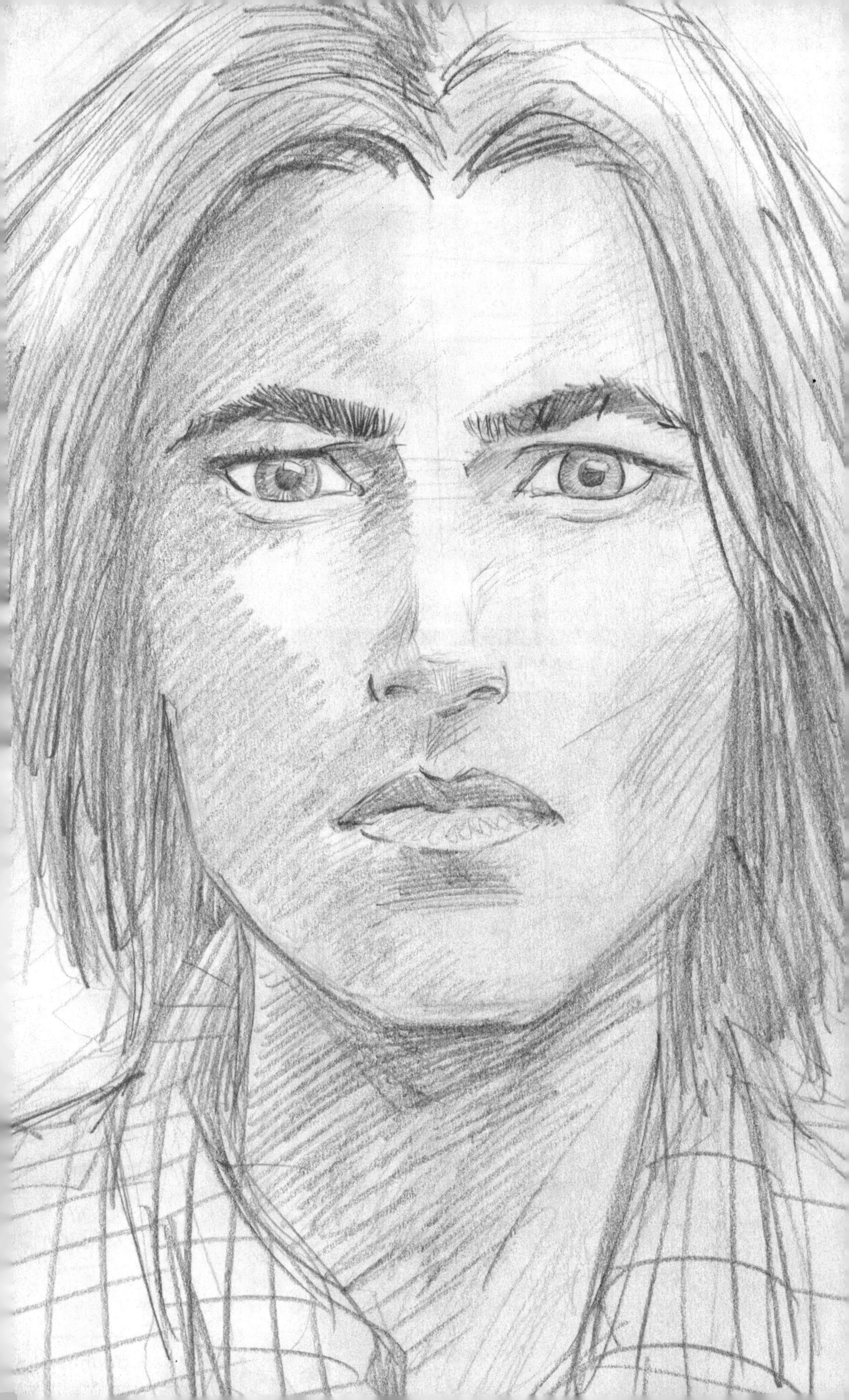

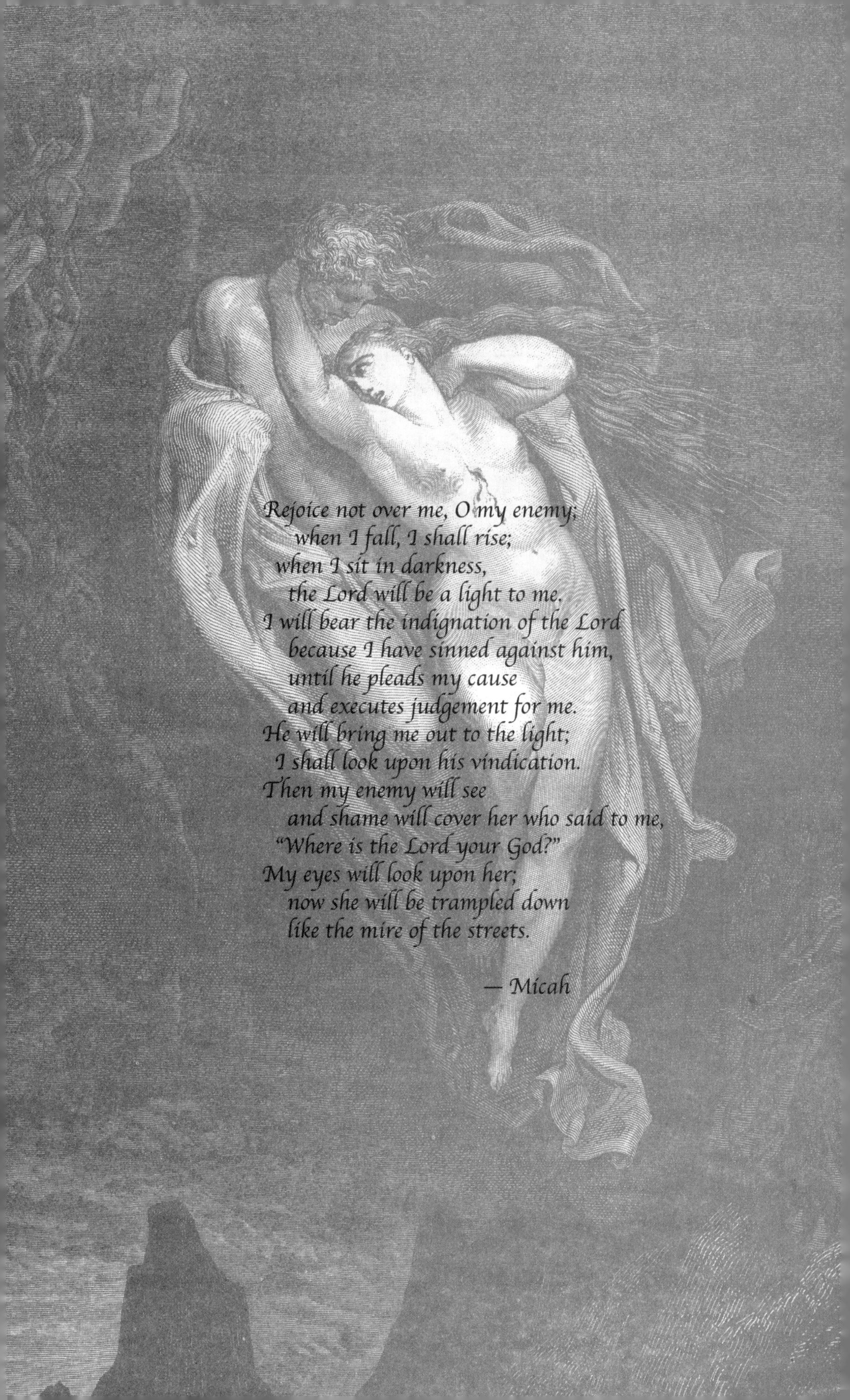

Rejoice not over me, O my enemy;
when I fall, I shall rise;
when I sit in darkness,
the Lord will be a light to me.
I will bear the indignation of the Lord
because I have sinned against him,
until he pleads my cause
and executes judgement for me.
He will bring me out to the light;
I shall look upon his vindication.
Then my enemy will see
and shame will cover her who said to me,
"Where is the Lord your God?"
My eyes will look upon her;
now she will be trampled down
like the mire of the streets.

— Micah

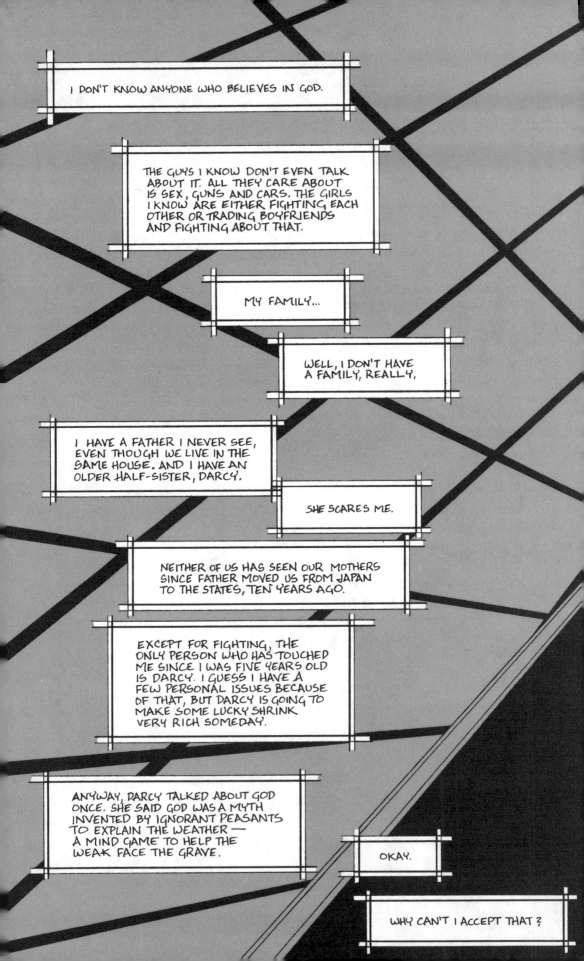

I DON'T KNOW ANYONE WHO BELIEVES IN GOD.

THE GUYS I KNOW DON'T EVEN TALK ABOUT IT. ALL THEY CARE ABOUT IS SEX, GUNS AND CARS. THE GIRLS I KNOW ARE EITHER FIGHTING EACH OTHER OR TRADING BOYFRIENDS AND FIGHTING ABOUT THAT.

MY FAMILY...

WELL, I DON'T HAVE A FAMILY, REALLY.

I HAVE A FATHER I NEVER SEE, EVEN THOUGH WE LIVE IN THE SAME HOUSE. AND I HAVE AN OLDER HALF-SISTER, DARCY.

SHE SCARES ME.

NEITHER OF US HAS SEEN OUR MOTHERS SINCE FATHER MOVED US FROM JAPAN TO THE STATES, TEN YEARS AGO.

EXCEPT FOR FIGHTING, THE ONLY PERSON WHO HAS TOUCHED ME SINCE I WAS FIVE YEARS OLD IS DARCY. I GUESS I HAVE A FEW PERSONAL ISSUES BECAUSE OF THAT, BUT DARCY IS GOING TO MAKE SOME LUCKY SHRINK VERY RICH SOMEDAY.

ANYWAY, DARCY TALKED ABOUT GOD ONCE. SHE SAID GOD WAS A MYTH INVENTED BY IGNORANT PEASANTS TO EXPLAIN THE WEATHER — A MIND GAME TO HELP THE WEAK FACE THE GRAVE.

OKAY.

WHY CAN'T I ACCEPT THAT?

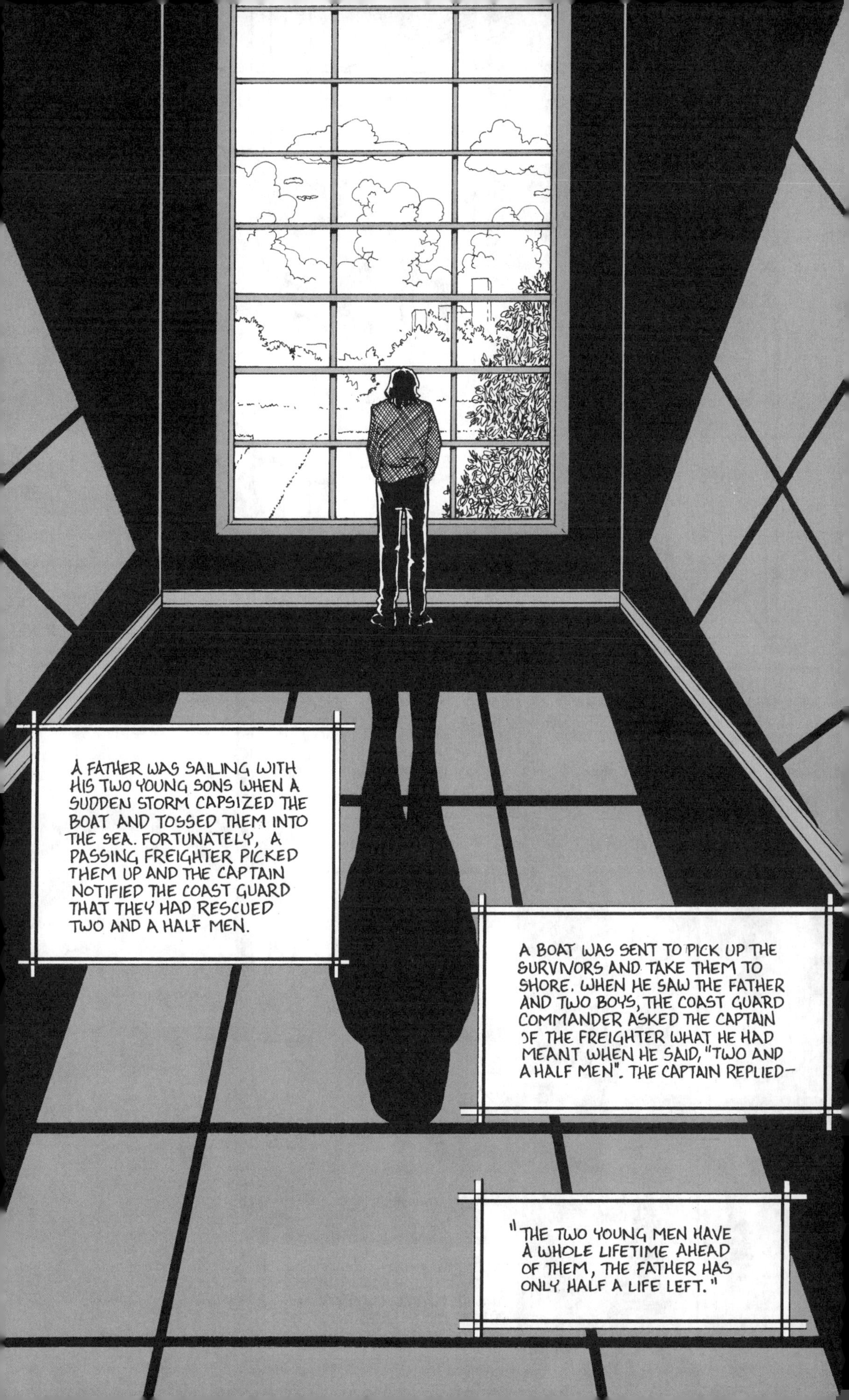
A FATHER WAS SAILING WITH HIS TWO YOUNG SONS WHEN A SUDDEN STORM CAPSIZED THE BOAT AND TOSSED THEM INTO THE SEA. FORTUNATELY, A PASSING FREIGHTER PICKED THEM UP AND THE CAPTAIN NOTIFIED THE COAST GUARD THAT THEY HAD RESCUED TWO AND A HALF MEN.
A BOAT WAS SENT TO PICK UP THE SURVIVORS AND TAKE THEM TO SHORE. WHEN HE SAW THE FATHER AND TWO BOYS, THE COAST GUARD COMMANDER ASKED THE CAPTAIN OF THE FREIGHTER WHAT HE HAD MEANT WHEN HE SAID, "TWO AND A HALF MEN". THE CAPTAIN REPLIED—
"THE TWO YOUNG MEN HAVE A WHOLE LIFETIME AHEAD OF THEM, THE FATHER HAS ONLY HALF A LIFE LEFT."

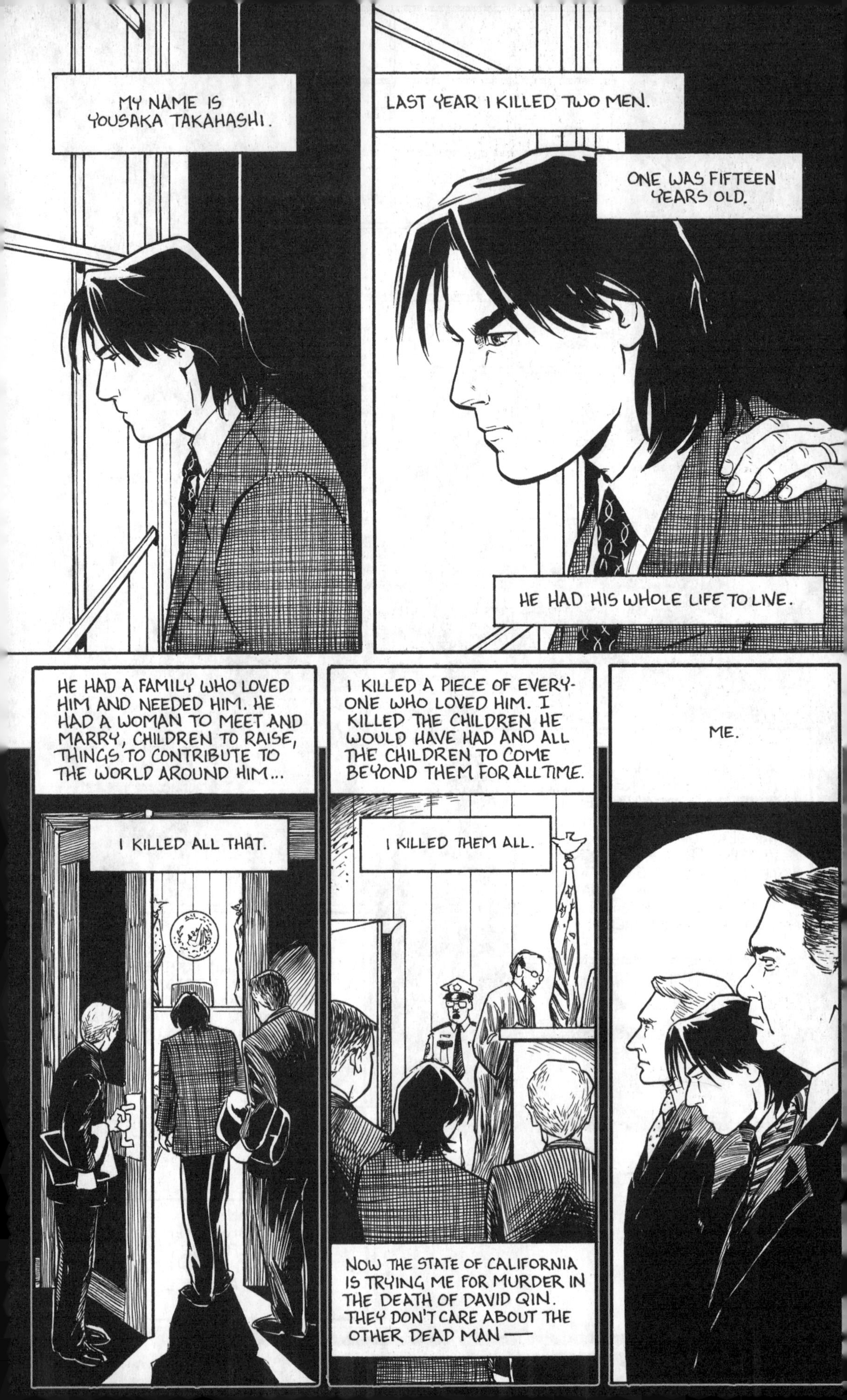
MY NAME IS YOUSAKA TAKAHASHI.
LAST YEAR I KILLED TWO MEN.
ONE WAS FIFTEEN YEARS OLD.
HE HAD HIS WHOLE LIFE TO LIVE.
HE HAD A FAMILY WHO LOVED HIM AND NEEDED HIM. HE HAD A WOMAN TO MEET AND MARRY, CHILDREN TO RAISE, THINGS TO CONTRIBUTE TO THE WORLD AROUND HIM...
I KILLED ALL THAT.
I KILLED A PIECE OF EVERY-ONE WHO LOVED HIM. I KILLED THE CHILDREN HE WOULD HAVE HAD AND ALL THE CHILDREN TO COME BEYOND THEM FOR ALL TIME.
I KILLED THEM ALL.
NOW THE STATE OF CALIFORNIA IS TRYING ME FOR MURDER IN THE DEATH OF DAVID QIN. THEY DON'T CARE ABOUT THE OTHER DEAD MAN —
ME.

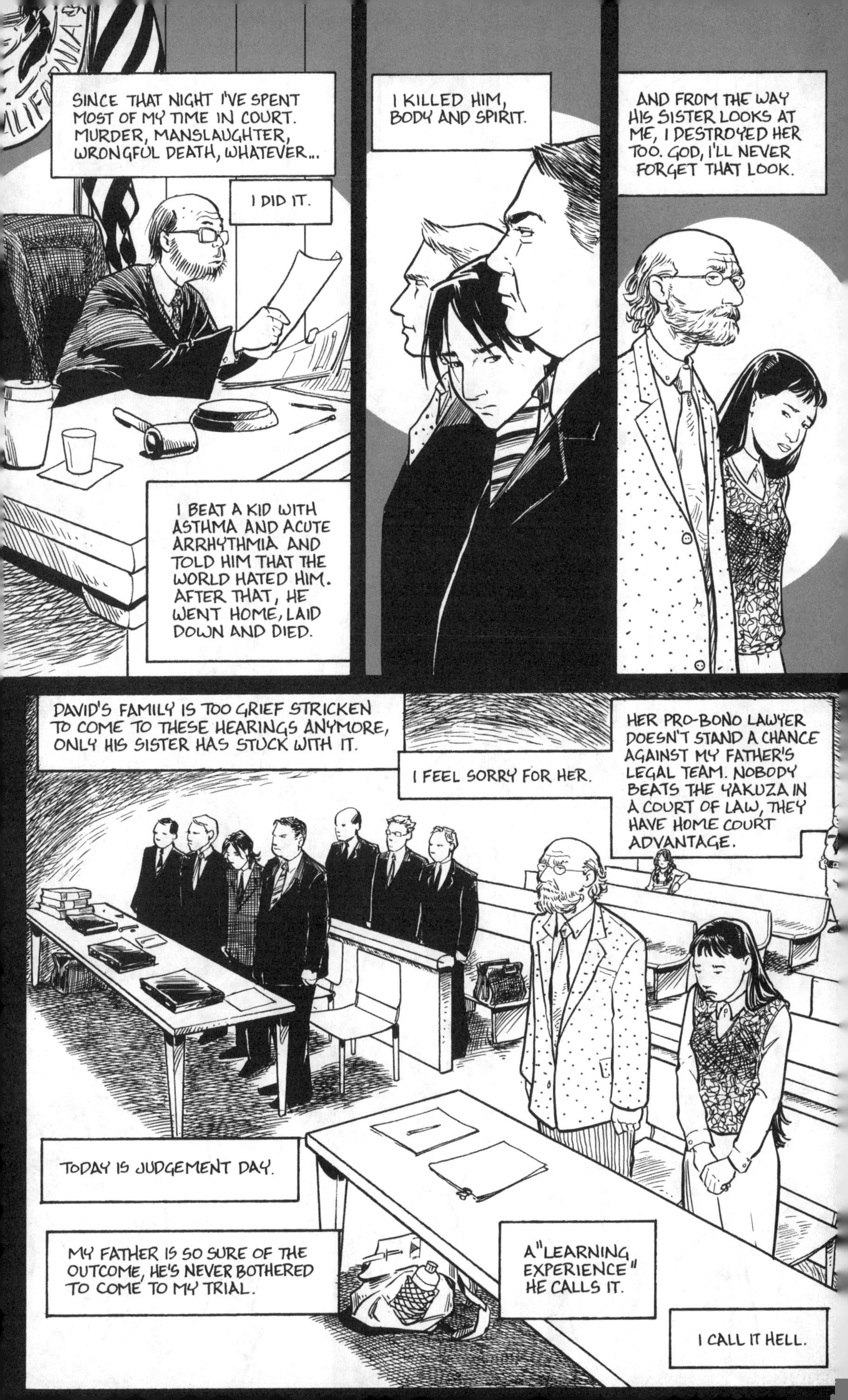
SINCE THAT NIGHT I'VE SPENT MOST OF MY TIME IN COURT. MURDER, MANSLAUGHTER, WRONGFUL DEATH, WHATEVER...
I DID IT.
I BEAT A KID WITH ASTHMA AND ACUTE ARRHYTHMIA AND TOLD HIM THAT THE WORLD HATED HIM. AFTER THAT, HE WENT HOME, LAID DOWN AND DIED.
I KILLED HIM, BODY AND SPIRIT.
AND FROM THE WAY HIS SISTER LOOKS AT ME, I DESTROYED HER TOO. GOD, I'LL NEVER FORGET THAT LOOK.
DAVID'S FAMILY IS TOO GRIEF STRICKEN TO COME TO THESE HEARINGS ANYMORE, ONLY HIS SISTER HAS STUCK WITH IT.
I FEEL SORRY FOR HER.
HER PRO-BONO LAWYER DOESN'T STAND A CHANCE AGAINST MY FATHER'S LEGAL TEAM. NOBODY BEATS THE YAKUZA IN A COURT OF LAW, THEY HAVE HOME COURT ADVANTAGE.
TODAY IS JUDGEMENT DAY.
MY FATHER IS SO SURE OF THE OUTCOME, HE'S NEVER BOTHERED TO COME TO MY TRIAL.
A "LEARNING EXPERIENCE" HE CALLS IT.
I CALL IT HELL.

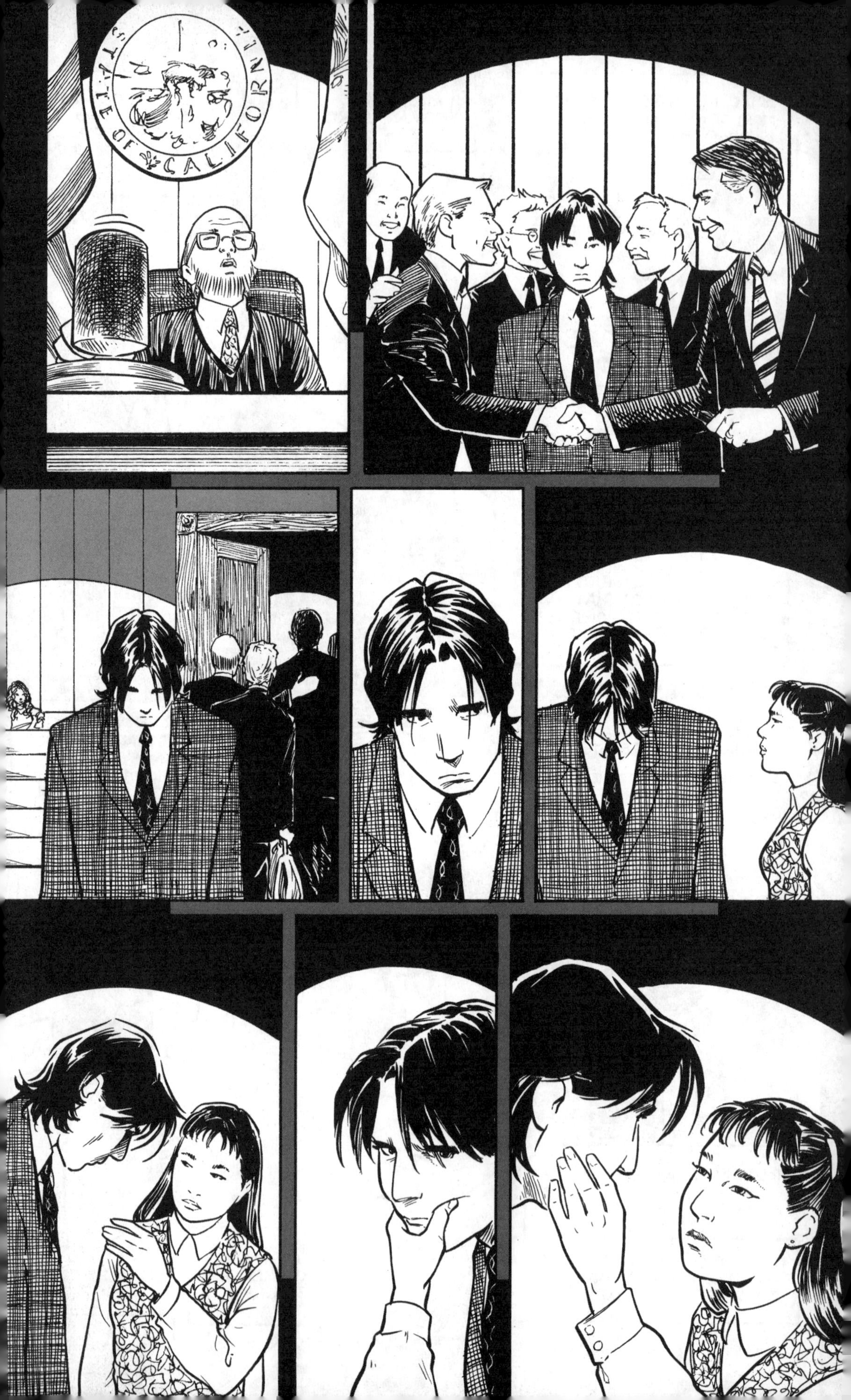
STATE OF CALIFORN

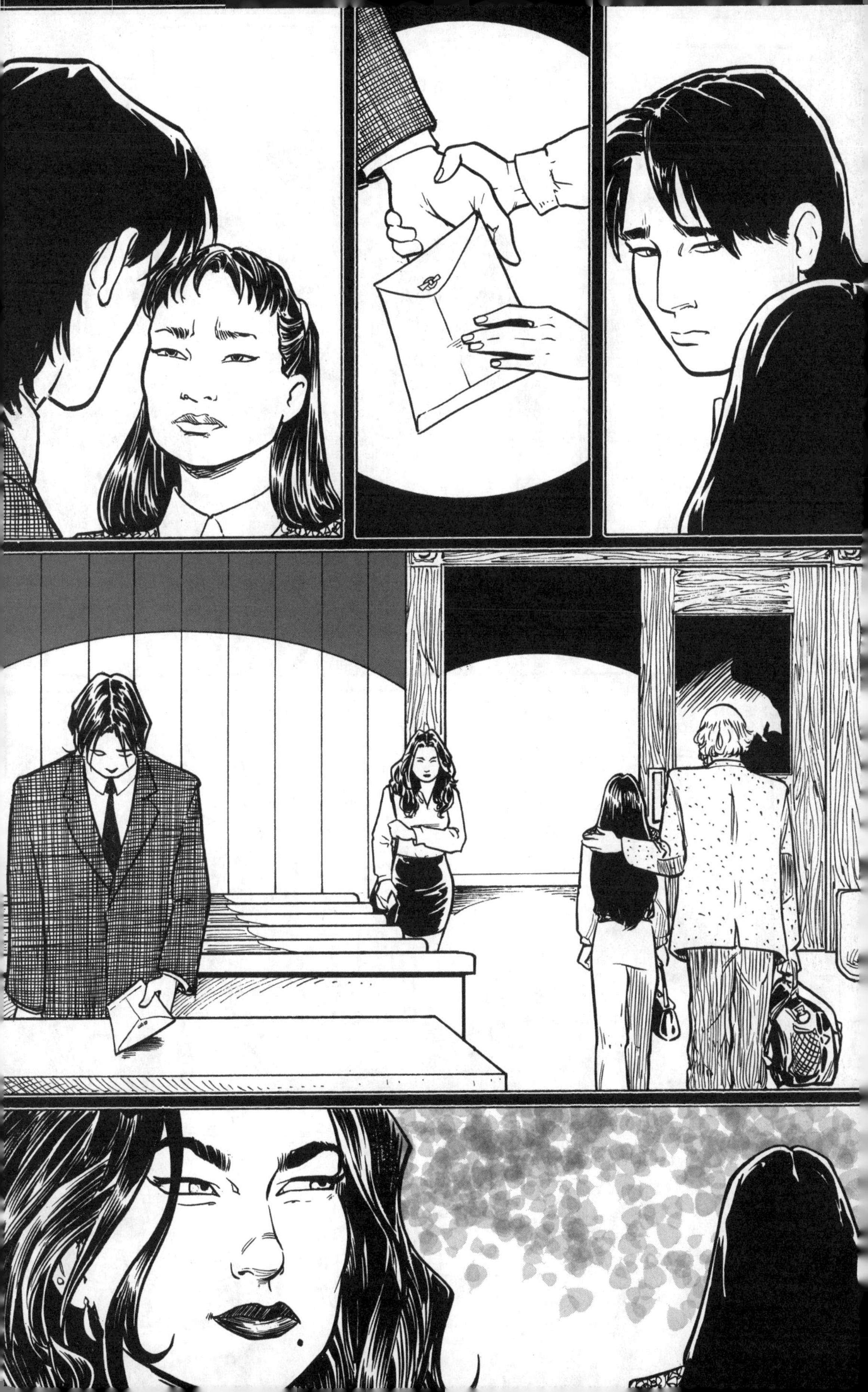

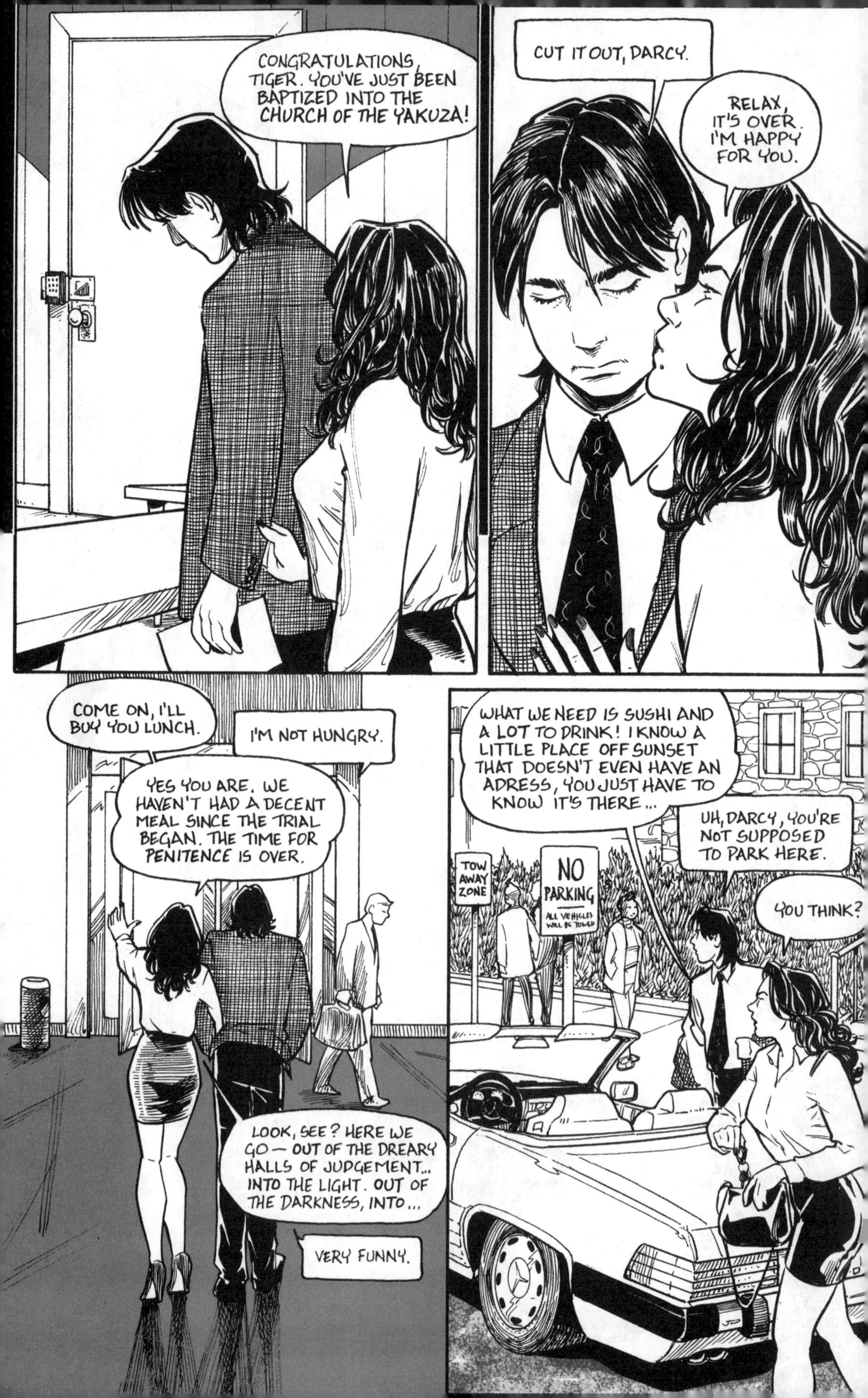
CONGRATULATIONS, TIGER. YOU'VE JUST BEEN BAPTIZED INTO THE CHURCH OF THE YAKUZA!
CUT IT OUT, DARCY.
RELAX, IT'S OVER. I'M HAPPY FOR YOU.
COME ON, I'LL BUY YOU LUNCH.
I'M NOT HUNGRY.
YES YOU ARE. WE HAVEN'T HAD A DECENT MEAL SINCE THE TRIAL BEGAN. THE TIME FOR PENITENCE IS OVER.
LOOK, SEE? HERE WE GO — OUT OF THE DREARY HALLS OF JUDGEMENT... INTO THE LIGHT. OUT OF THE DARKNESS, INTO...
VERY FUNNY.
WHAT WE NEED IS SUSHI AND A LOT TO DRINK! I KNOW A LITTLE PLACE OFF SUNSET THAT DOESN'T EVEN HAVE AN ADRESS, YOU JUST HAVE TO KNOW IT'S THERE...
TOW AWAY ZONE
NO PARKING
ALL VEHICLES WILL BE TOWED
UH, DARCY, YOU'RE NOT SUPPOSED TO PARK HERE.
YOU THINK?

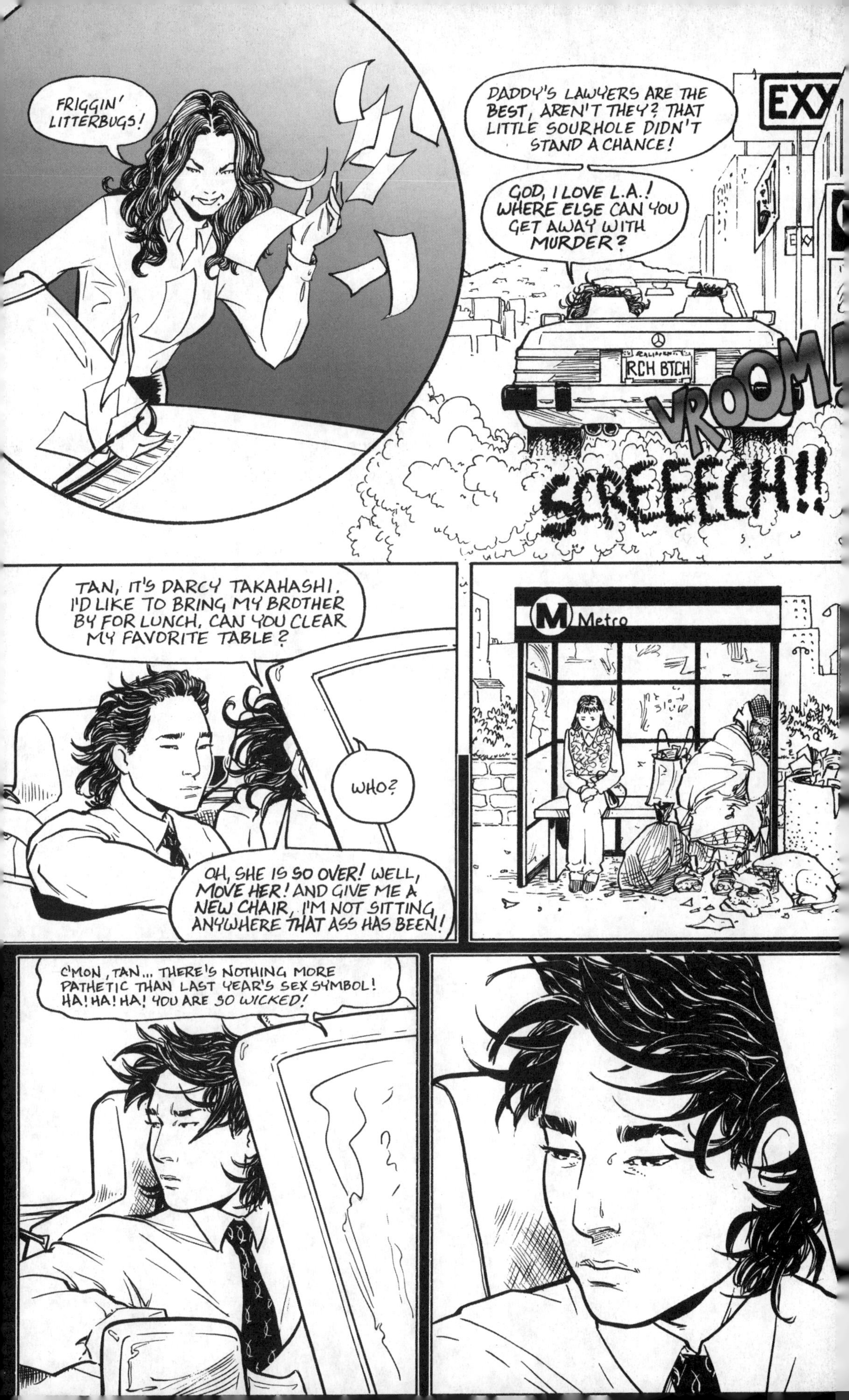
FRIGGIN' LITTERBUGS!
DADDY'S LAWYERS ARE THE BEST, AREN'T THEY? THAT LITTLE SOURHOLE DIDN'T STAND A CHANCE!
GOD, I LOVE L.A.! WHERE ELSE CAN YOU GET AWAY WITH MURDER?
RCH BTCH
VROOM!
SCREEECH!!
TAN, IT'S DARCY TAKAHASHI. I'D LIKE TO BRING MY BROTHER BY FOR LUNCH, CAN YOU CLEAR MY FAVORITE TABLE?
WHO?
OH, SHE IS SO OVER! WELL, MOVE HER! AND GIVE ME A NEW CHAIR, I'M NOT SITTING ANYWHERE THAT ASS HAS BEEN!
Metro
C'MON, TAN... THERE'S NOTHING MORE PATHETIC THAN LAST YEAR'S SEX SYMBOL! HA! HA! HA! YOU ARE SO WICKED!

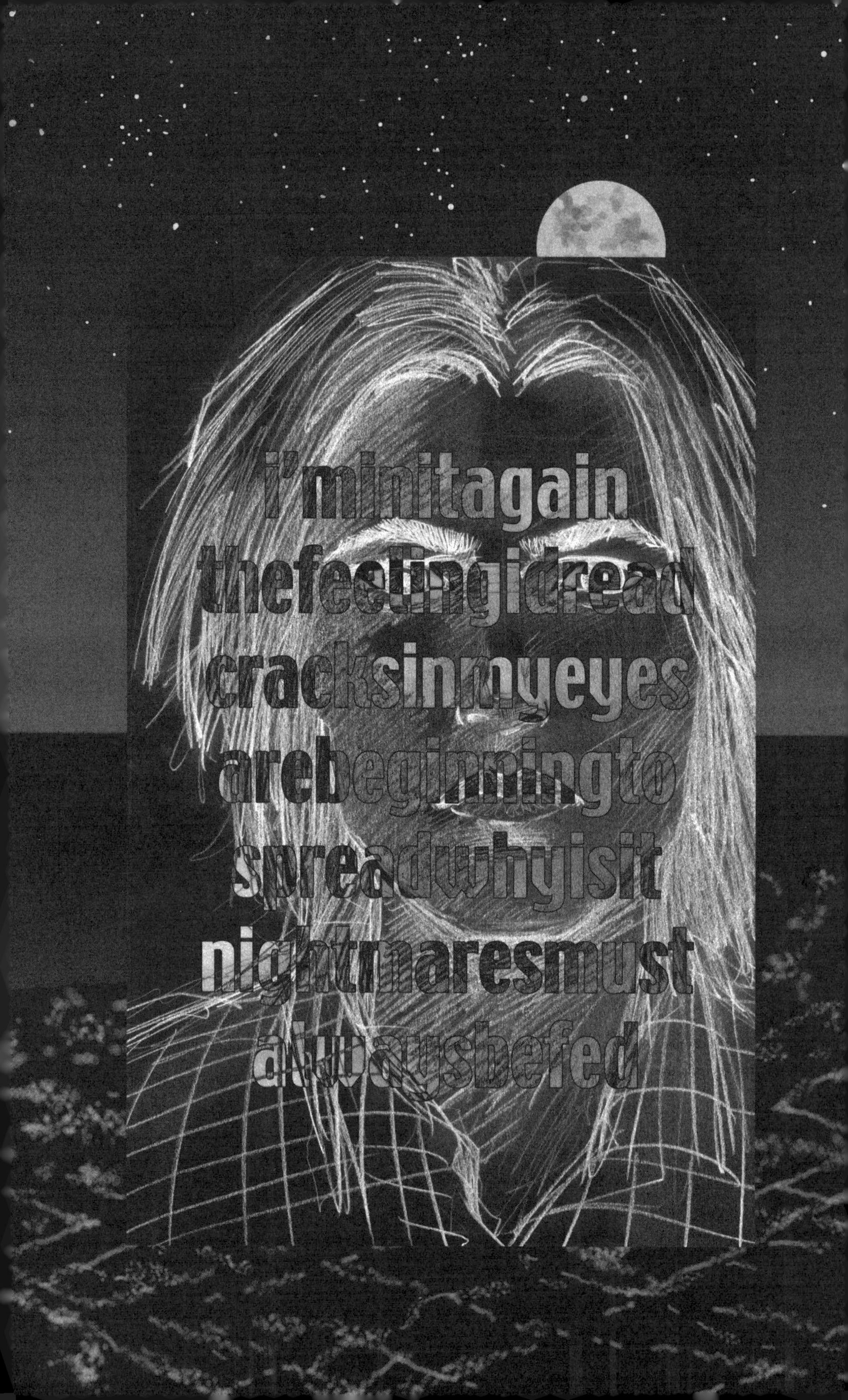
i'minitagain
thefeelingidread
cracksinmyeyes
arebeginningto
spreadwhyisit
nightmaresmust
alwaysbefed

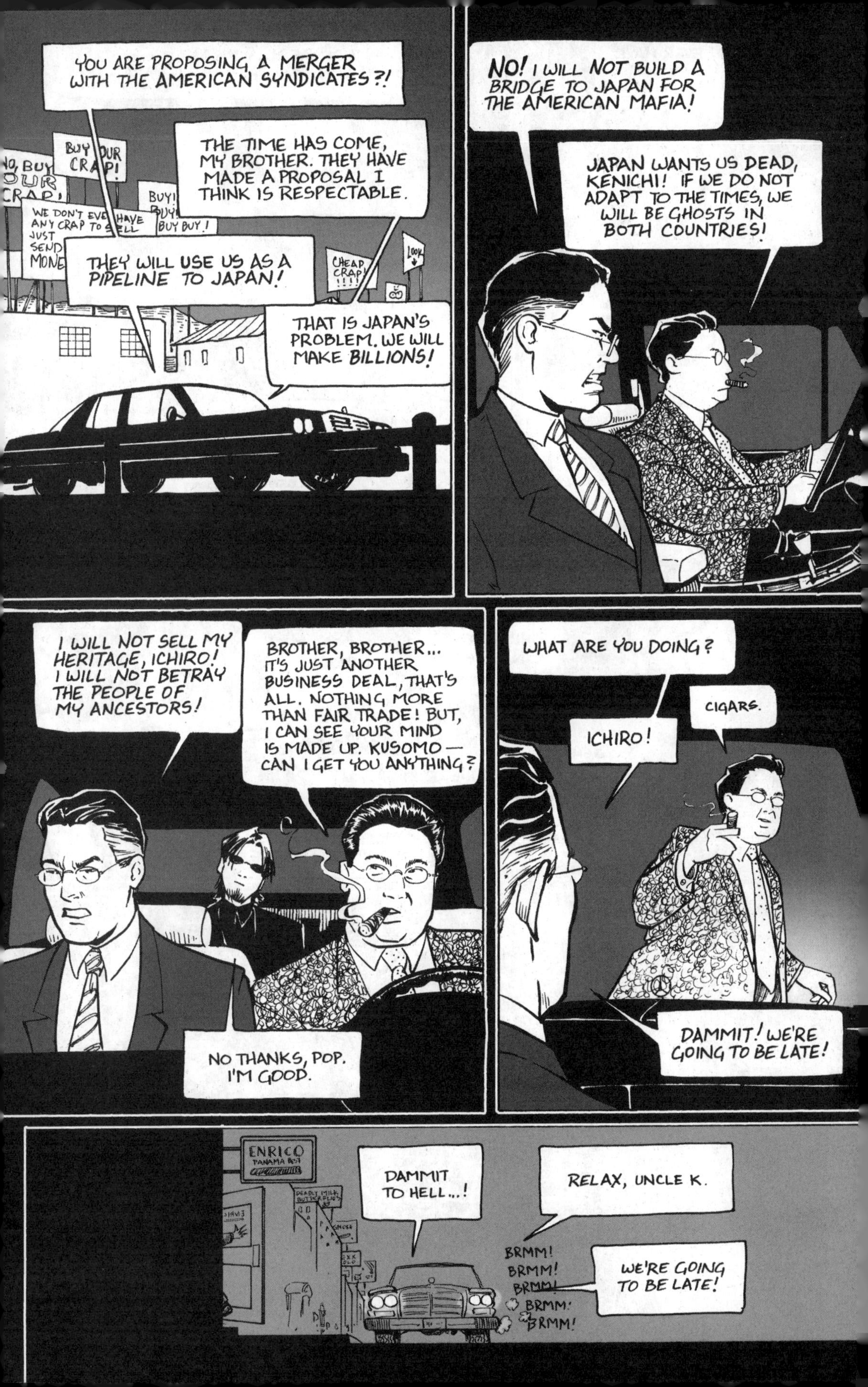
YOU ARE PROPOSING A MERGER WITH THE AMERICAN SYNDICATES?!
BUY YOUR CRAP!
NO, BUY OUR CRAP!
WE DON'T EVEN HAVE ANY CRAP TO SELL JUST SEND MONE
BUY! BUY! BUY BUY!
CHEAP CRAP! !!!!
LOOK
THE TIME HAS COME, MY BROTHER. THEY HAVE MADE A PROPOSAL I THINK IS RESPECTABLE.
THEY WILL USE US AS A PIPELINE TO JAPAN!
THAT IS JAPAN'S PROBLEM. WE WILL MAKE BILLIONS!
NO! I WILL NOT BUILD A BRIDGE TO JAPAN FOR THE AMERICAN MAFIA!
JAPAN WANTS US DEAD, KENICHI! IF WE DO NOT ADAPT TO THE TIMES, WE WILL BE GHOSTS IN BOTH COUNTRIES!
I WILL NOT SELL MY HERITAGE, ICHIRO! I WILL NOT BETRAY THE PEOPLE OF MY ANCESTORS!
BROTHER, BROTHER... IT'S JUST ANOTHER BUSINESS DEAL, THAT'S ALL. NOTHING MORE THAN FAIR TRADE! BUT, I CAN SEE YOUR MIND IS MADE UP. KUSOMO— CAN I GET YOU ANYTHING?
NO THANKS, POP. I'M GOOD.
WHAT ARE YOU DOING?
ICHIRO!
CIGARS.
DAMMIT! WE'RE GOING TO BE LATE!
ENRICO
DAMMIT TO HELL...!
RELAX, UNCLE K.
BRMM! BRMM! BRMM! BRMM! BRMM!
WE'RE GOING TO BE LATE!

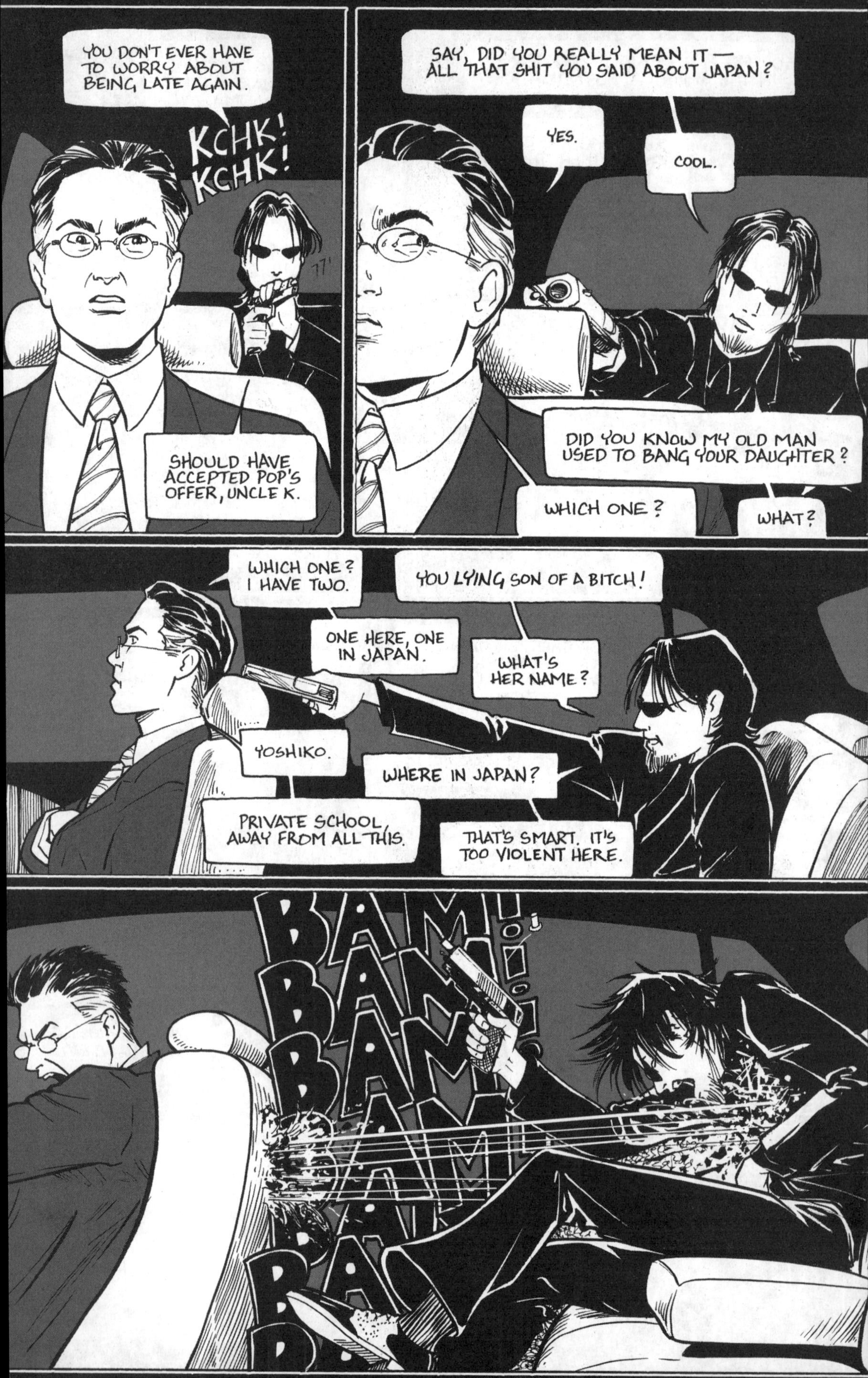
YOU DON'T EVER HAVE TO WORRY ABOUT BEING LATE AGAIN.
KCHK! KCHK!
SHOULD HAVE ACCEPTED POP'S OFFER, UNCLE K.
SAY, DID YOU REALLY MEAN IT — ALL THAT SHIT YOU SAID ABOUT JAPAN?
YES.
COOL.
DID YOU KNOW MY OLD MAN USED TO BANG YOUR DAUGHTER?
WHICH ONE?
WHAT?
WHICH ONE? I HAVE TWO.
ONE HERE, ONE IN JAPAN.
YOU LYING SON OF A BITCH!
WHAT'S HER NAME?
YOSHIKO.
WHERE IN JAPAN?
PRIVATE SCHOOL AWAY FROM ALL THIS.
THAT'S SMART. IT'S TOO VIOLENT HERE.
BAM! BAM! BAM! BAM! BAM!

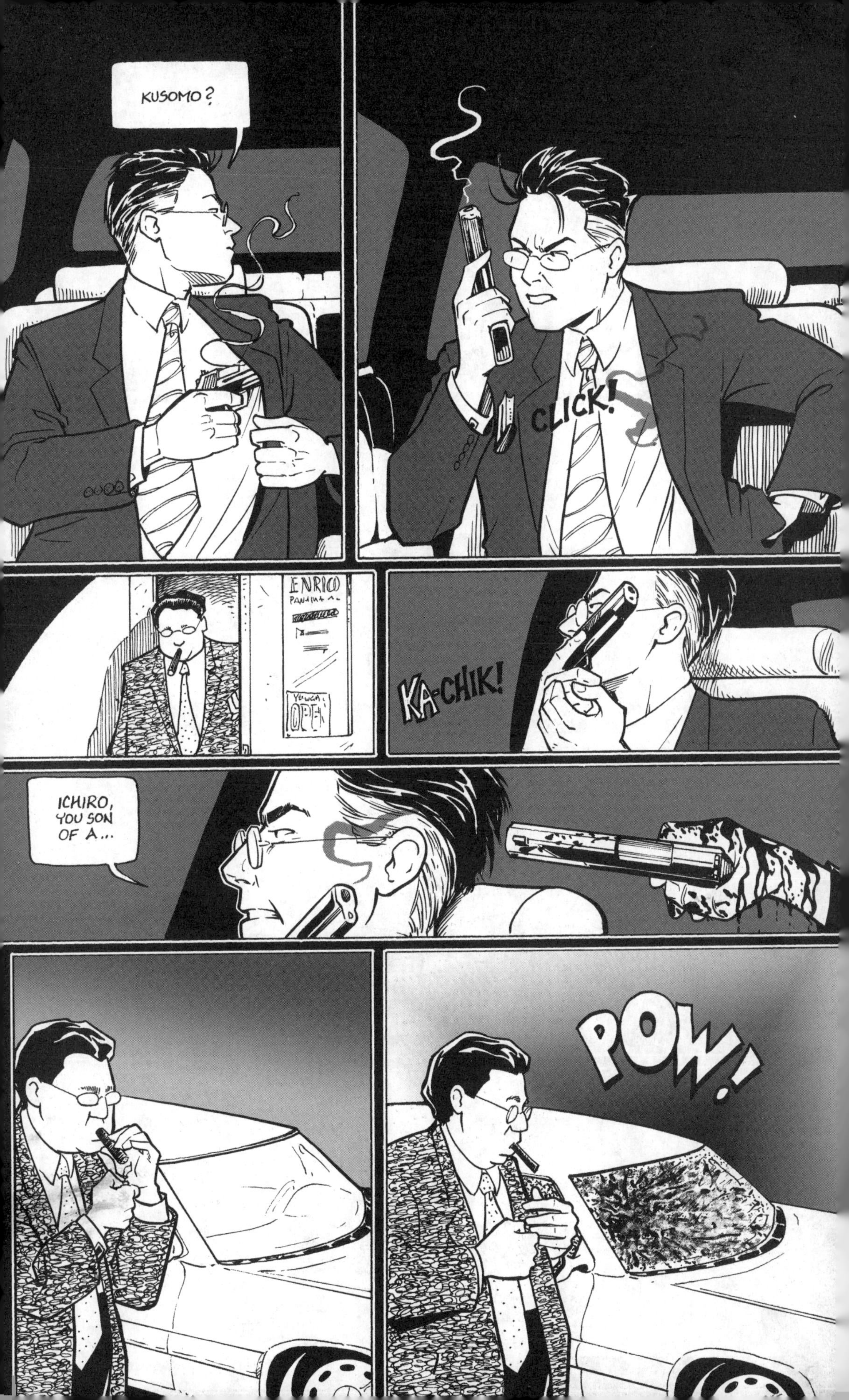
KUSOMO?
CLICK!
ENRICO
KA-CHIK!
ICHIRO, YOU SON OF A...
POW!

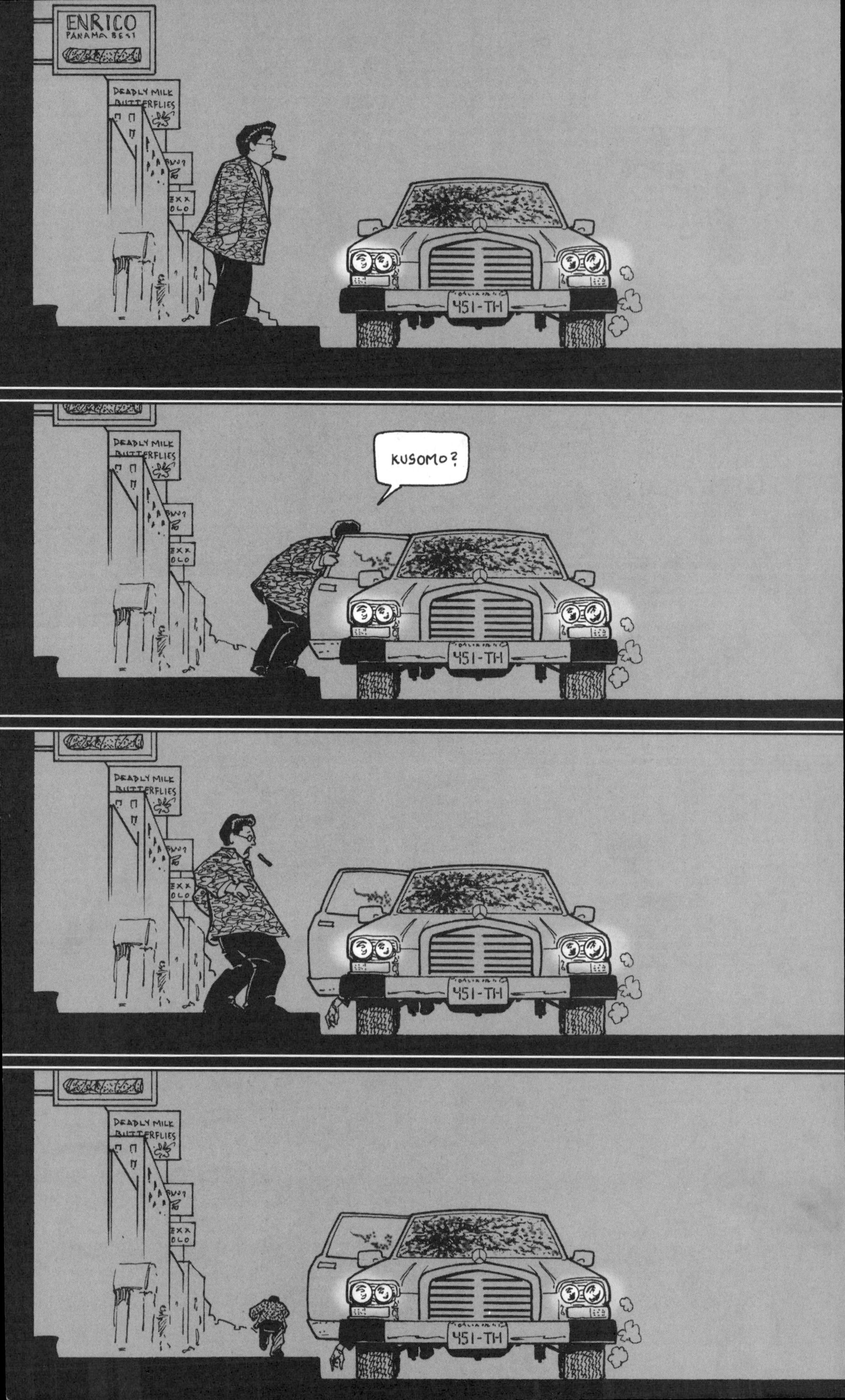
ENRICO
PANAMA BEST
DEADLY MILK BUTTERFLIES
451-TH
DEADLY MILK BUTTERFLIES
KUSOMO?
451-TH
DEADLY MILK BUTTERFLIES
451-TH
DEADLY MILK BUTTERFLIES
451-TH

Oh that you were like a brother to me
who nursed at my mother's breasts!
If I found you outside, I would kiss you,
and none would despise me.
I would lead you and bring you
into the house of my mother—
she who used to teach me.
I would give you spiced wine to drink
the juice of my pomegranate.
I adjure you, O daughters of Jerusalem,
that you not stir up or awaken love until it pleases.
Set me as a seal upon your heart, as a seal upon your arm,
for love is strong as death, jealousy is fierce as the grave.

—Song Of Solomon

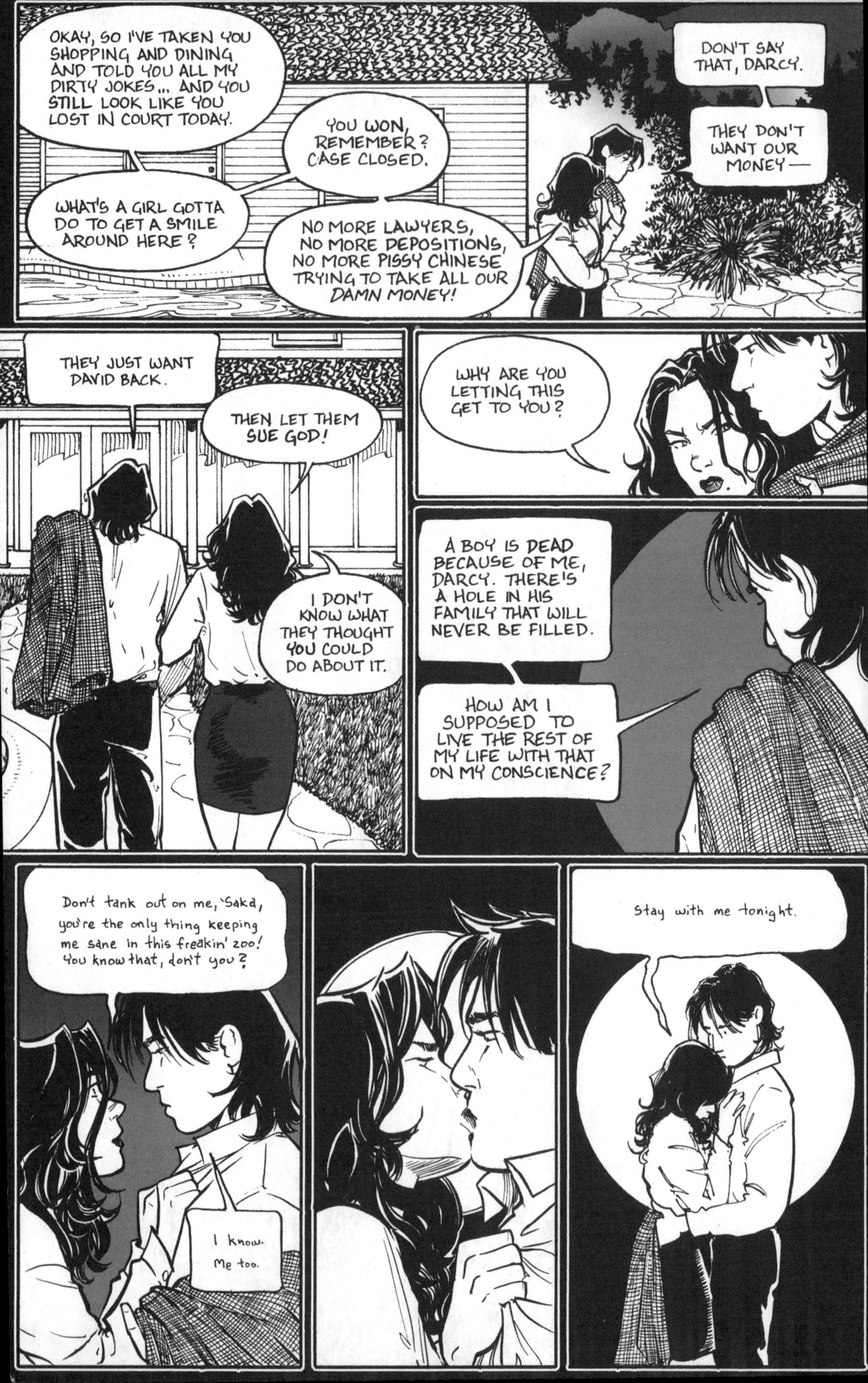
OKAY, SO I'VE TAKEN YOU SHOPPING AND DINING AND TOLD YOU ALL MY DIRTY JOKES... AND YOU STILL LOOK LIKE YOU LOST IN COURT TODAY.
WHAT'S A GIRL GOTTA DO TO GET A SMILE AROUND HERE?
YOU WON, REMEMBER? CASE CLOSED.
NO MORE LAWYERS, NO MORE DEPOSITIONS, NO MORE PISSY CHINESE TRYING TO TAKE ALL OUR DAMN MONEY!
DON'T SAY THAT, DARCY.
THEY DON'T WANT OUR MONEY—
THEY JUST WANT DAVID BACK.
THEN LET THEM SUE GOD!
I DON'T KNOW WHAT THEY THOUGHT YOU COULD DO ABOUT IT.
WHY ARE YOU LETTING THIS GET TO YOU?
A BOY IS DEAD BECAUSE OF ME, DARCY. THERE'S A HOLE IN HIS FAMILY THAT WILL NEVER BE FILLED.
HOW AM I SUPPOSED TO LIVE THE REST OF MY LIFE WITH THAT ON MY CONSCIENCE?
Don't tank out on me, 'Saka, you're the only thing keeping me sane in this freakin' zoo! You know that, don't you?
I know. Me too.
Stay with me tonight.

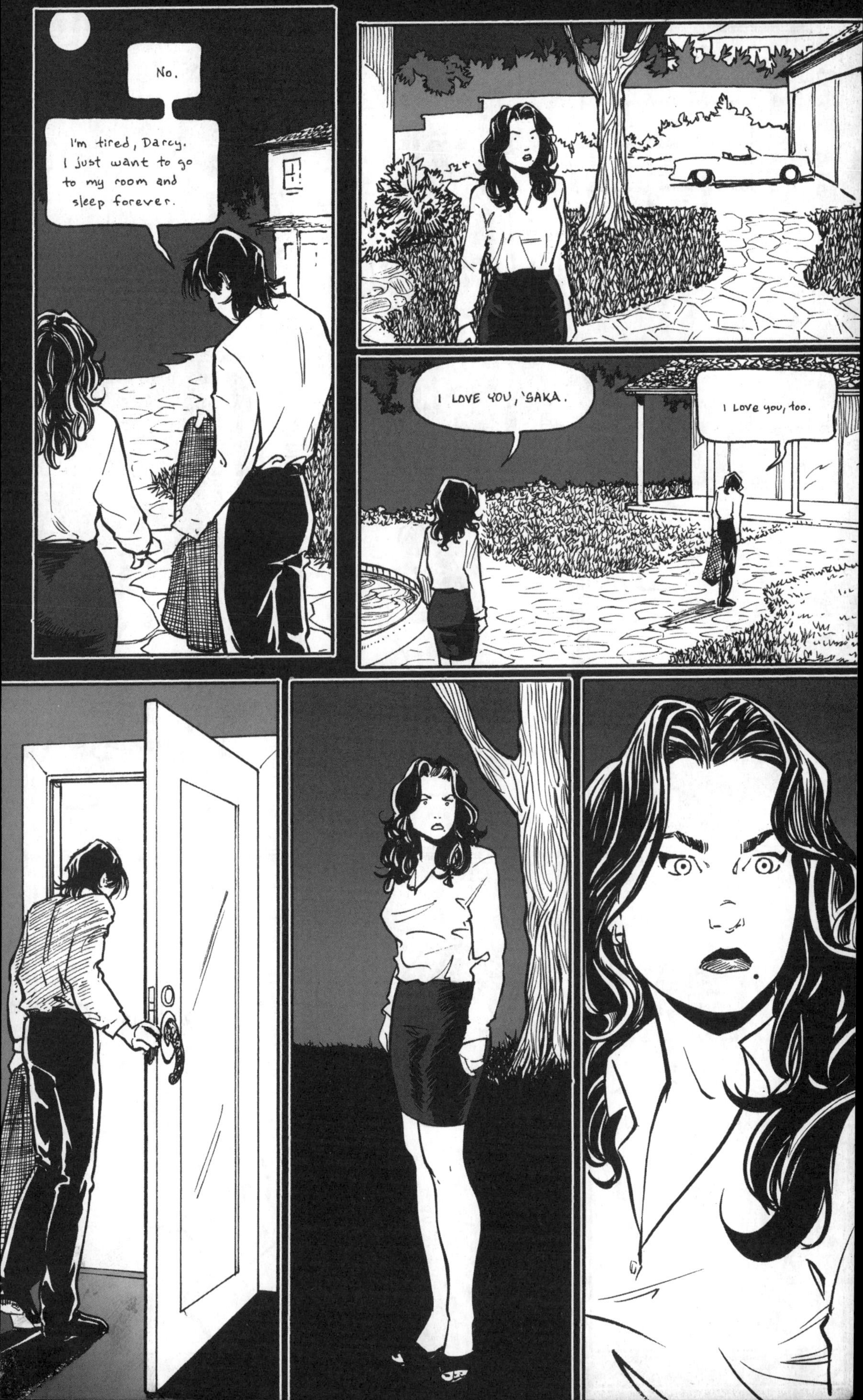
No.
I'm tired, Darcy. I just want to go to my room and sleep forever.
I LOVE YOU, 'SAKA.
I Love you, too.

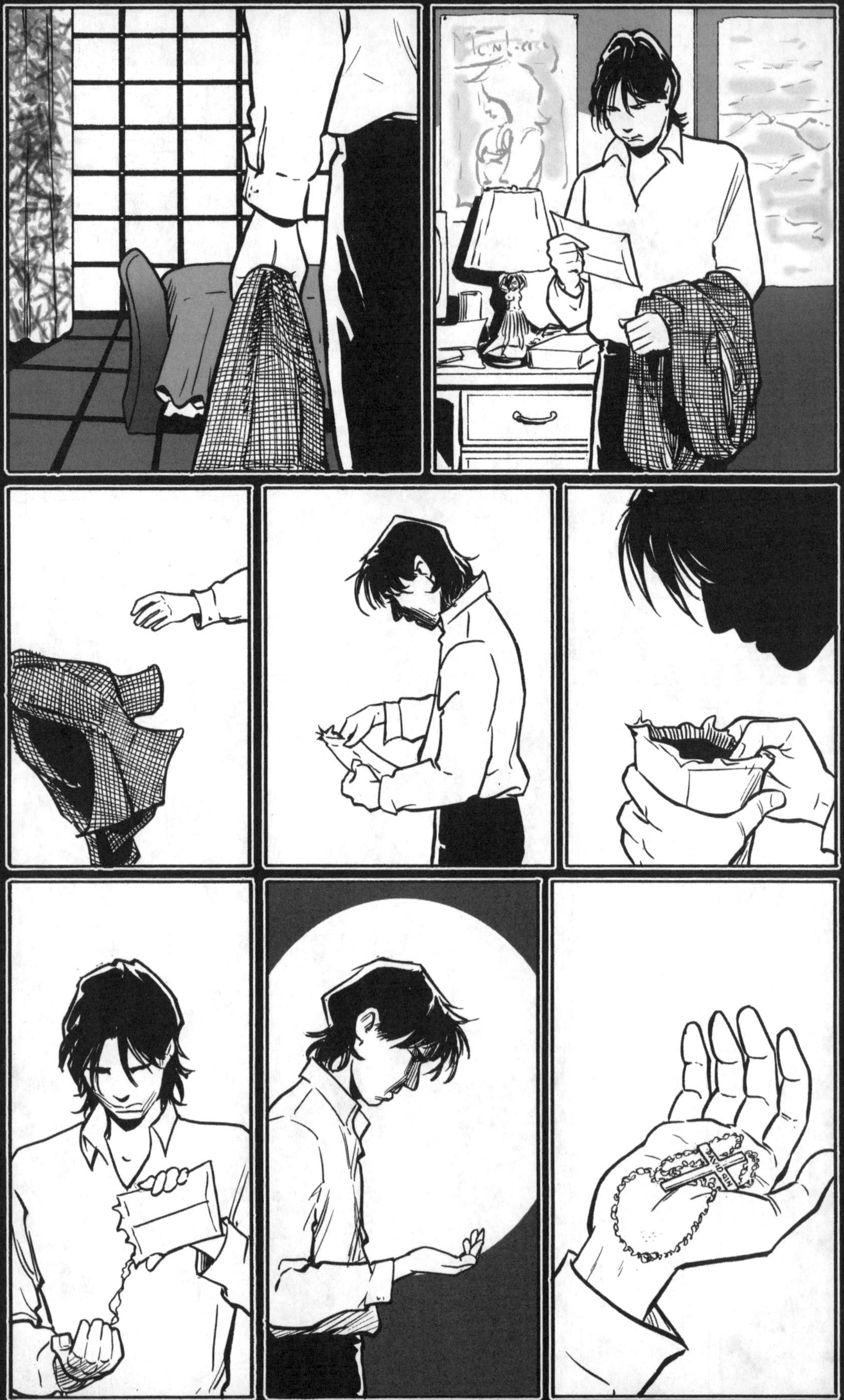

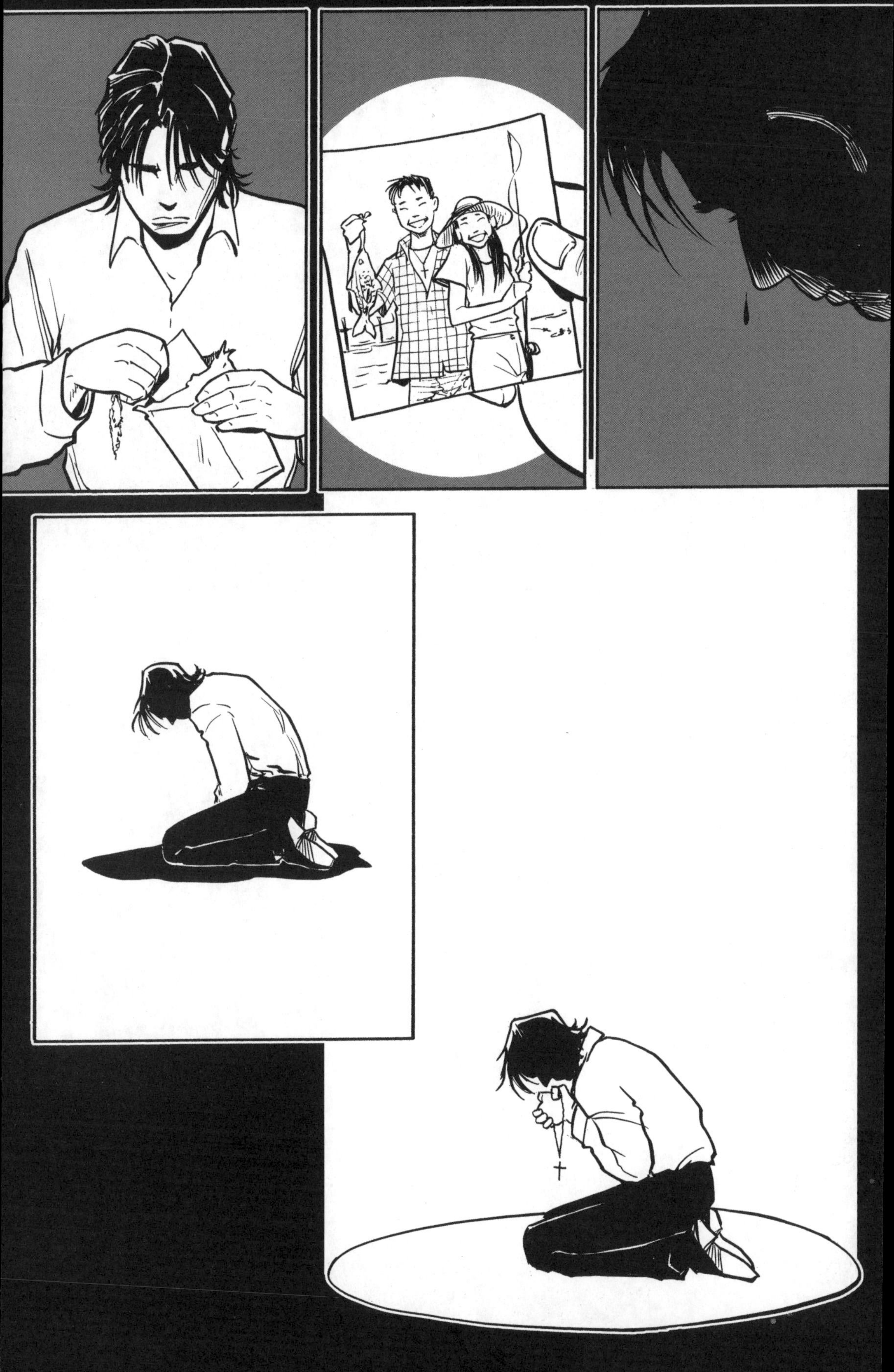

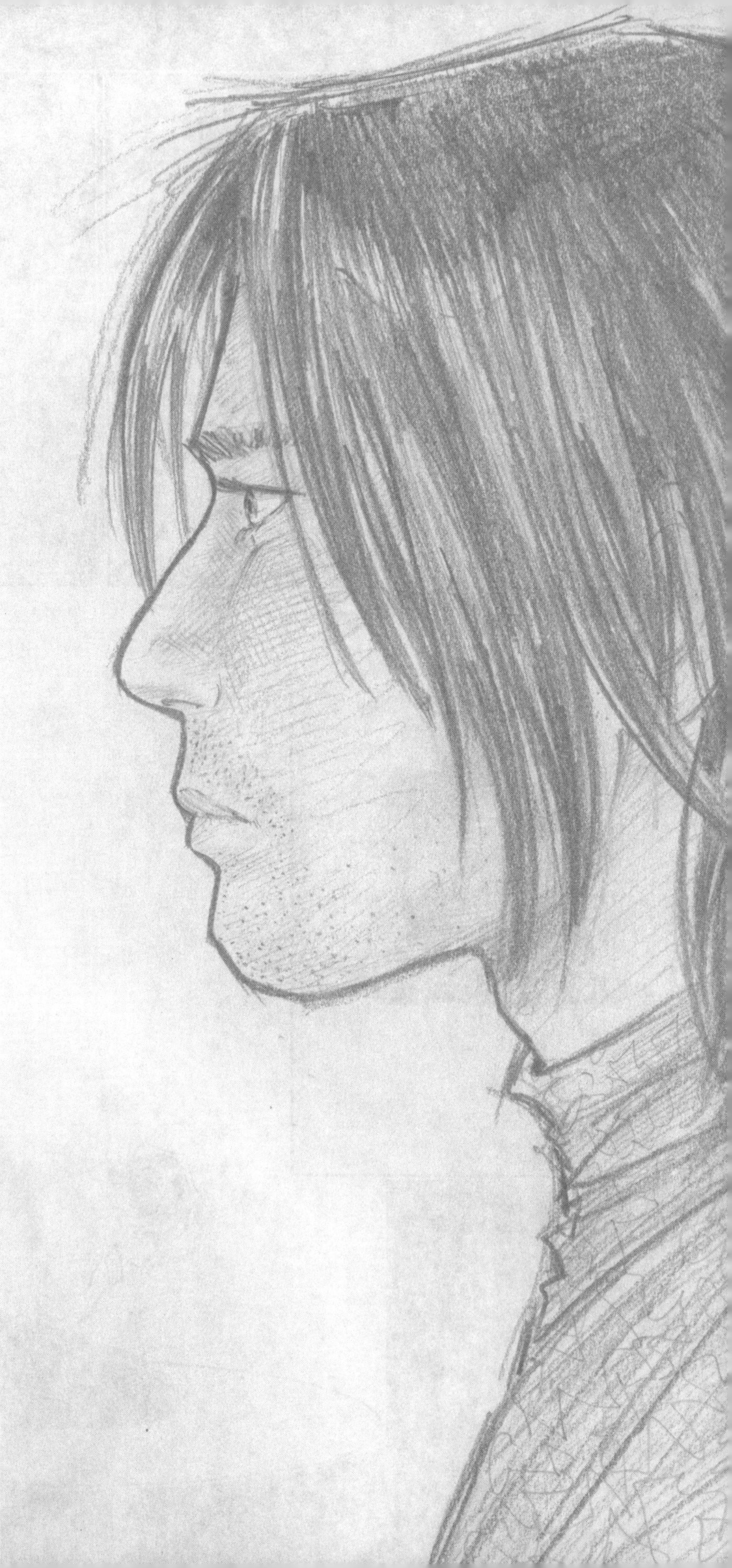

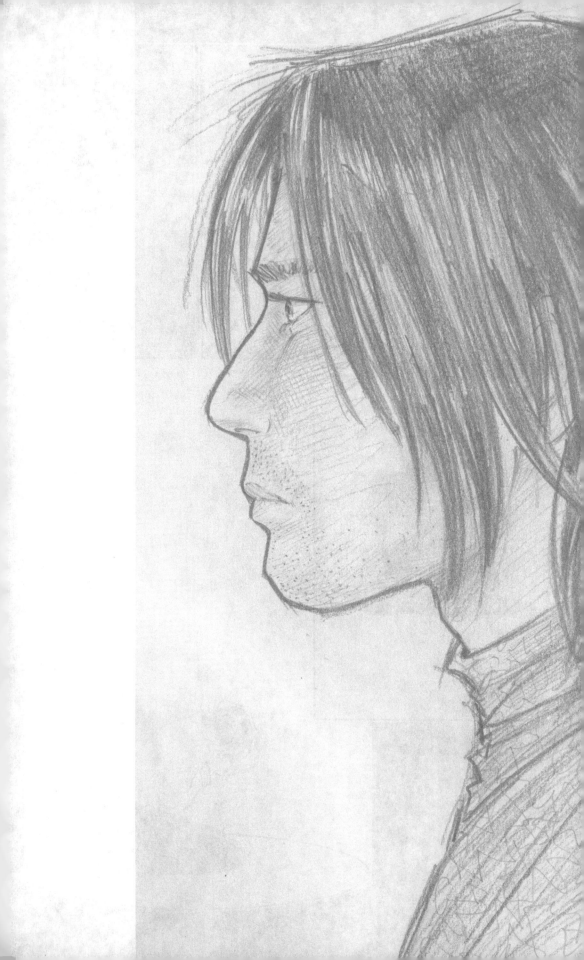

In arrogance the wicked hotly pursue the poor;
For the wicked boasts of the desires of his soul,
and the one greedy for gain
curses and renounces the Lord.
In the pride of his face the wicked does not seek him;
all his thoughts are, "There is no God."
He says in his heart, "I shall not be moved."
His mouth is filled with cursing and deceit and oppression;
under his tongue are mischief and iniquity.
He says in his heart, "God has forgotten,
He has hidden His face, He will never see it."

—Psalm 10

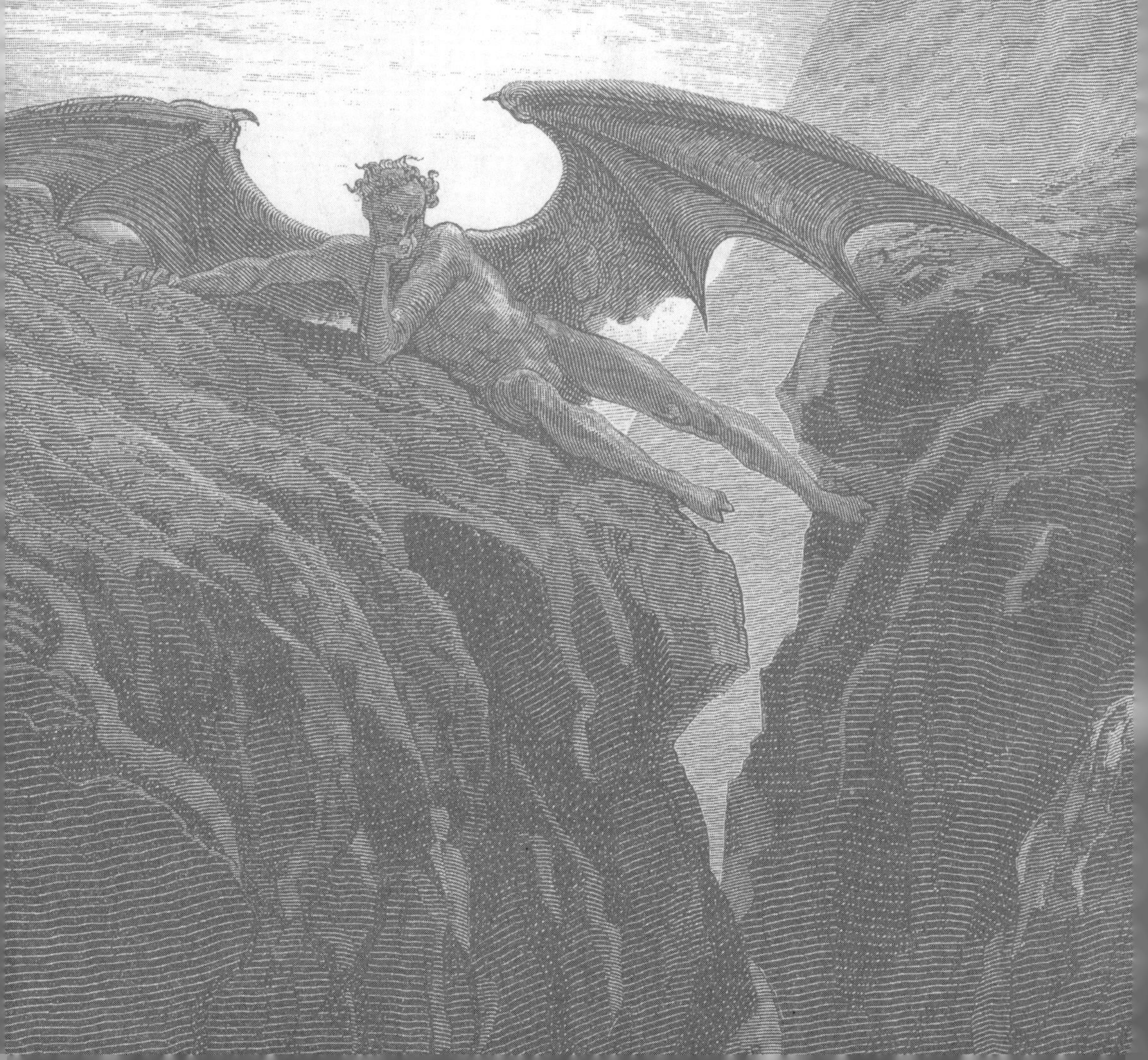

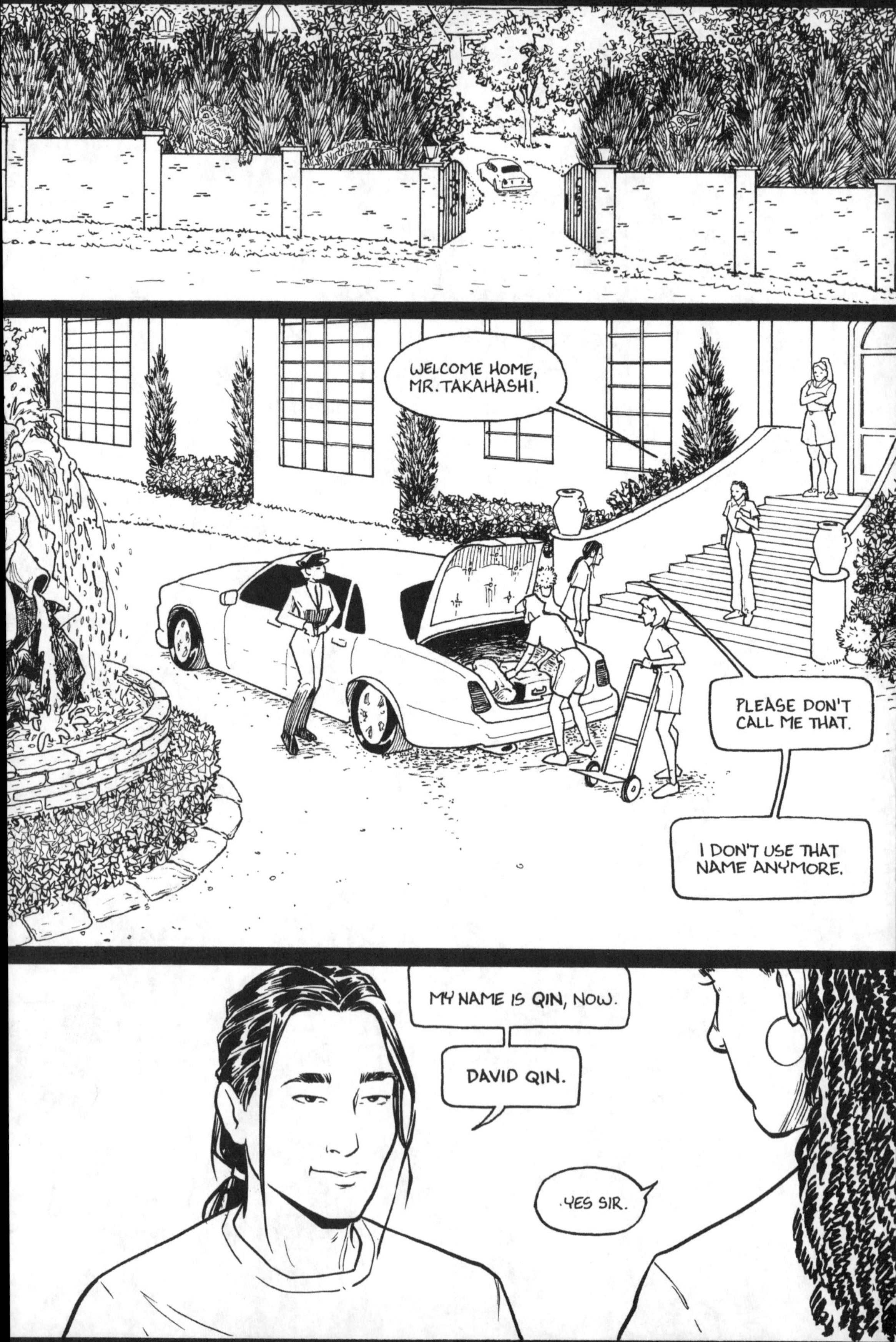
WELCOME HOME, MR. TAKAHASHI.
PLEASE DON'T CALL ME THAT.
I DON'T USE THAT NAME ANYMORE.
MY NAME IS QIN, NOW.
DAVID QIN.
.YES SIR.

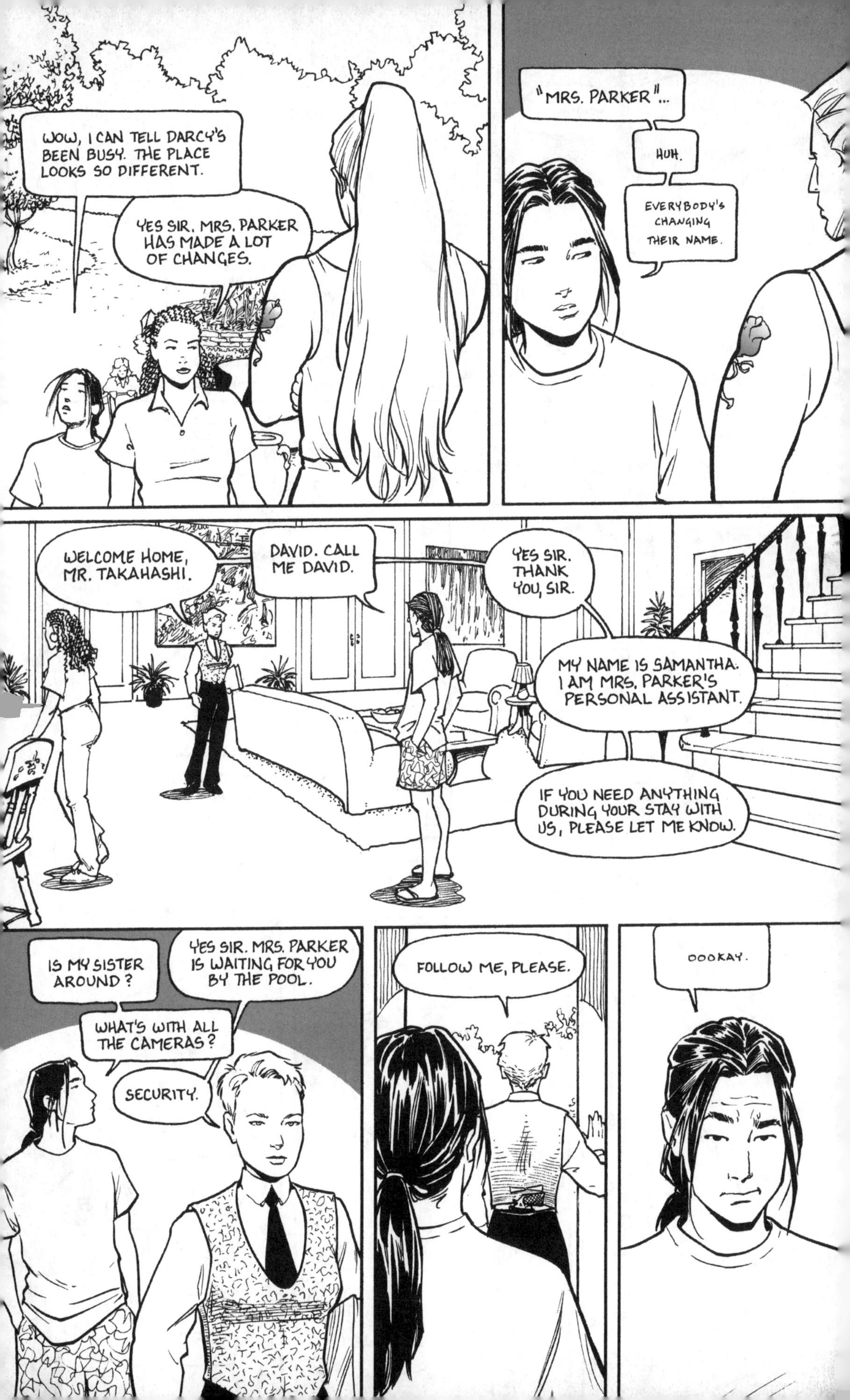
WOW, I CAN TELL DARCY'S BEEN BUSY. THE PLACE LOOKS SO DIFFERENT.
YES SIR. MRS. PARKER HAS MADE A LOT OF CHANGES.
"MRS. PARKER"...
HUH.
EVERYBODY'S CHANGING THEIR NAME.
WELCOME HOME, MR. TAKAHASHI.
DAVID. CALL ME DAVID.
YES SIR. THANK YOU, SIR.
MY NAME IS SAMANTHA. I AM MRS. PARKER'S PERSONAL ASSISTANT.
IF YOU NEED ANYTHING DURING YOUR STAY WITH US, PLEASE LET ME KNOW.
IS MY SISTER AROUND?
YES SIR. MRS. PARKER IS WAITING FOR YOU BY THE POOL.
WHAT'S WITH ALL THE CAMERAS?
SECURITY.
FOLLOW ME, PLEASE.
OOOKAY.

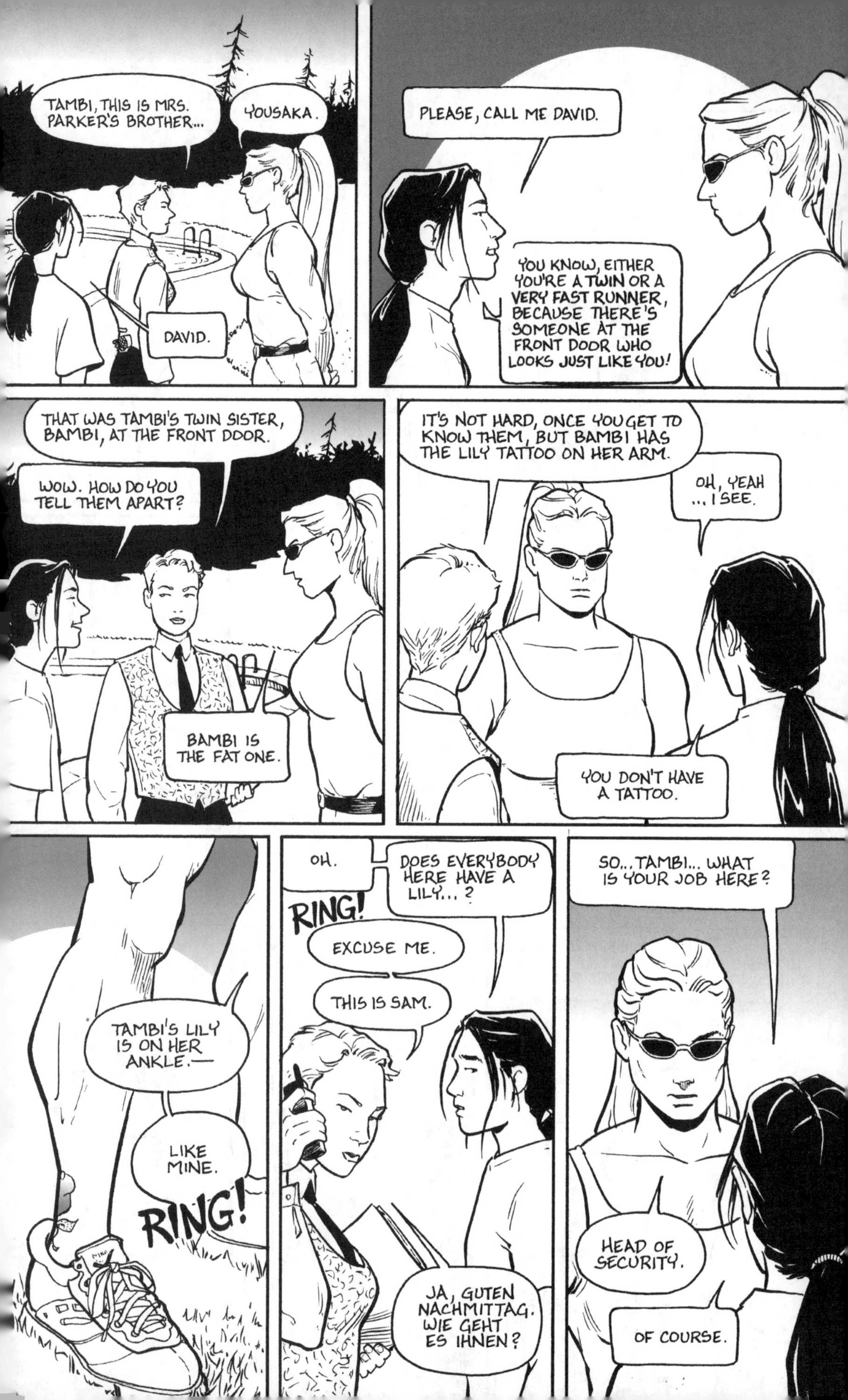
TAMBI, THIS IS MRS. PARKER'S BROTHER...
YOUSAKA.
DAVID.
PLEASE, CALL ME DAVID.
YOU KNOW, EITHER YOU'RE A TWIN OR A VERY FAST RUNNER, BECAUSE THERE'S SOMEONE AT THE FRONT DOOR WHO LOOKS JUST LIKE YOU!
THAT WAS TAMBI'S TWIN SISTER, BAMBI, AT THE FRONT DOOR.
WOW. HOW DO YOU TELL THEM APART?
BAMBI IS THE FAT ONE.
IT'S NOT HARD, ONCE YOU GET TO KNOW THEM, BUT BAMBI HAS THE LILY TATTOO ON HER ARM.
OH, YEAH ...I SEE.
YOU DON'T HAVE A TATTOO.
TAMBI'S LILY IS ON HER ANKLE.—
LIKE MINE.
RING!
OH.
DOES EVERYBODY HERE HAVE A LILY... ?
RING!
EXCUSE ME.
THIS IS SAM.
JA, GUTEN NACHMITTAG. WIE GEHT ES IHNEN?
SO... TAMBI... WHAT IS YOUR JOB HERE?
HEAD OF SECURITY.
OF COURSE.

For the lips of a forbidden woman drip honey, and her speech is smoother than oil,
But in the end she is bitter as wormwood, sharp as a two-edged sword.
Her feet go down to death; her steps follow the path to Hell;
She does not ponder the path of life; her ways wander, and she does not know it.

~Proverbs

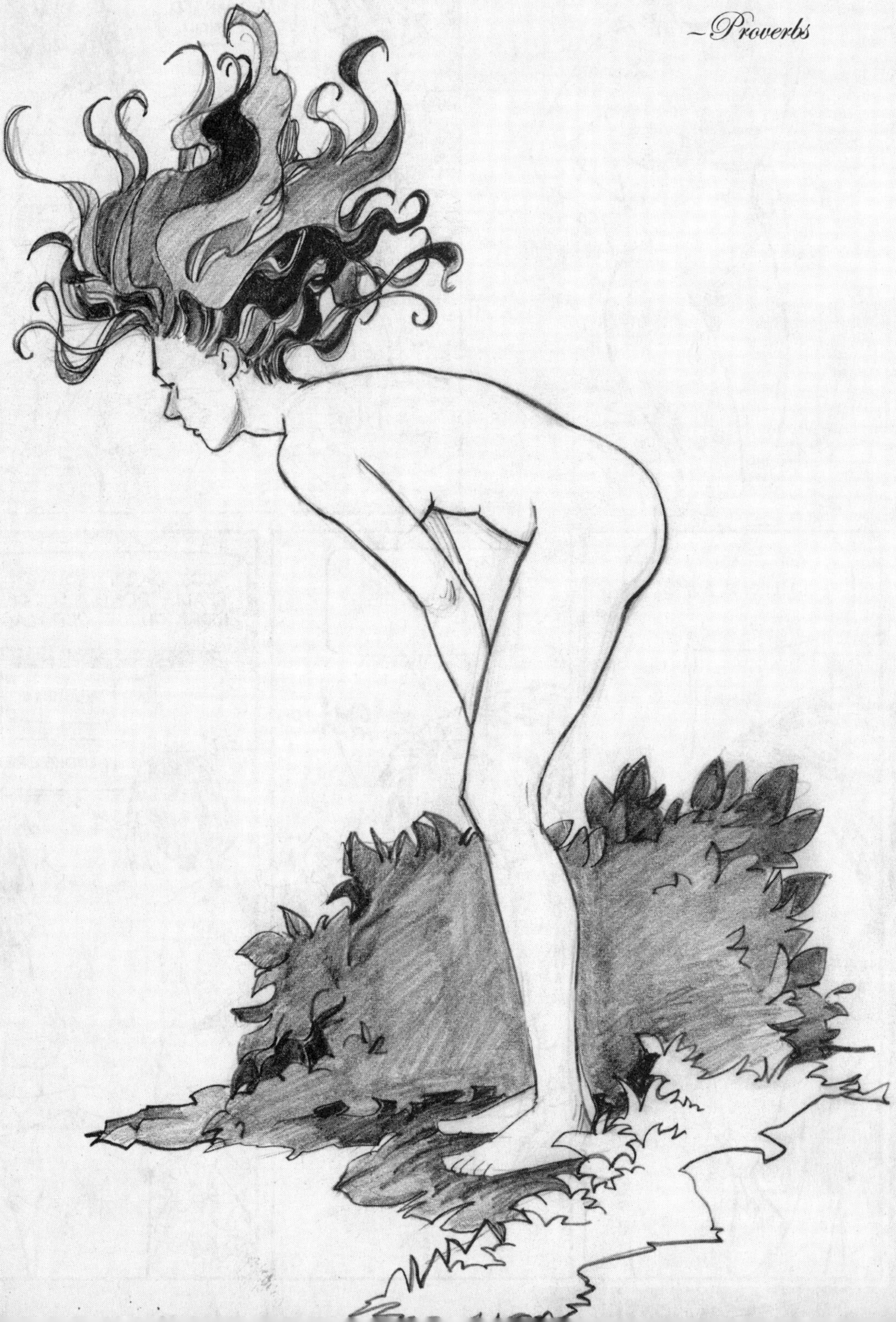

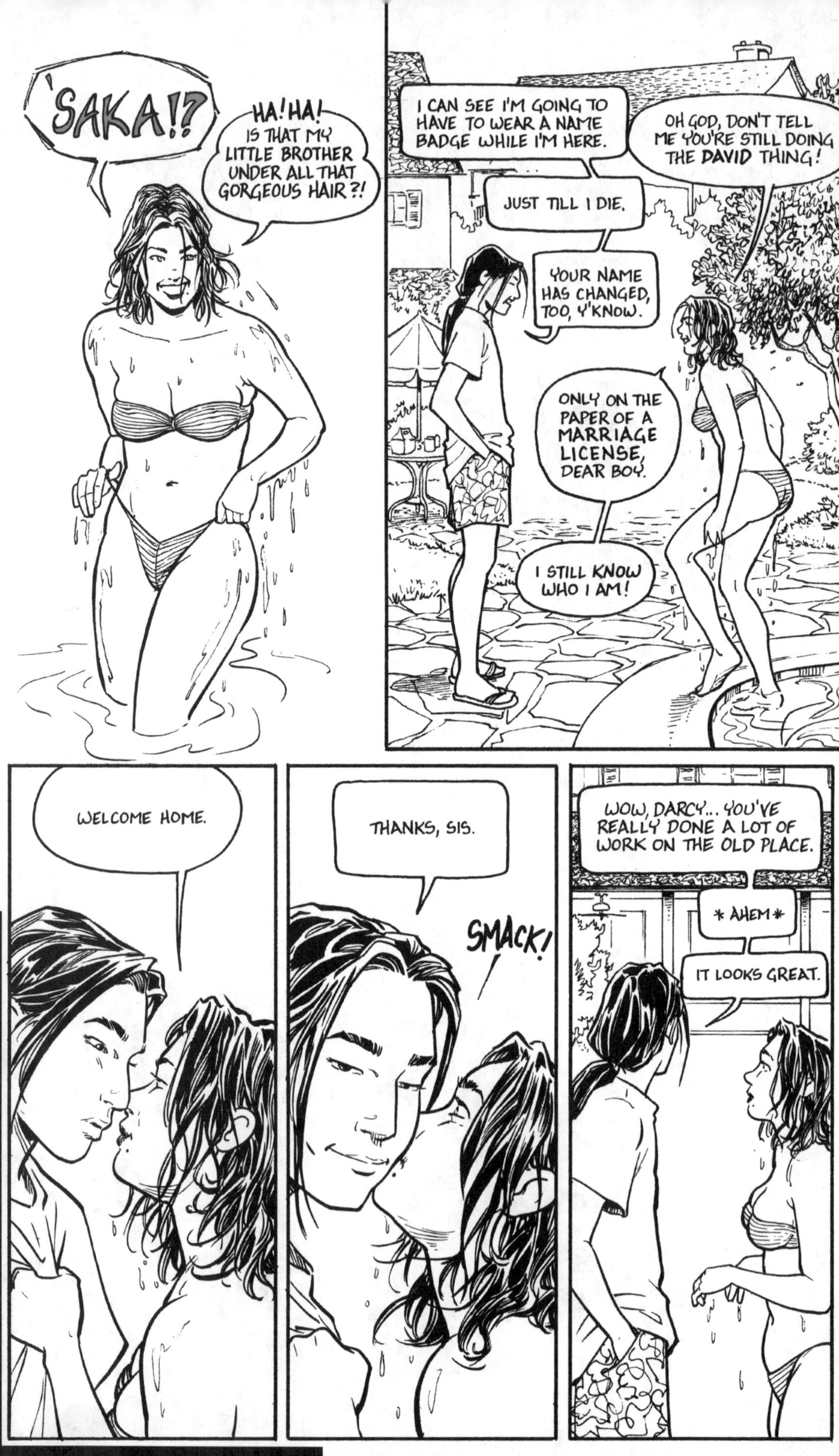
SAKA!?
HA! HA! IS THAT MY LITTLE BROTHER UNDER ALL THAT GORGEOUS HAIR?!
I CAN SEE I'M GOING TO HAVE TO WEAR A NAME BADGE WHILE I'M HERE.
JUST TILL I DIE.
OH GOD, DON'T TELL ME YOU'RE STILL DOING THE DAVID THING!
YOUR NAME HAS CHANGED, TOO, Y'KNOW.
ONLY ON THE PAPER OF A MARRIAGE LICENSE, DEAR BOY.
I STILL KNOW WHO I AM!
WELCOME HOME.
THANKS, SIS.
SMACK!
WOW, DARCY... YOU'VE REALLY DONE A LOT OF WORK ON THE OLD PLACE.
* AHEM *
IT LOOKS GREAT.

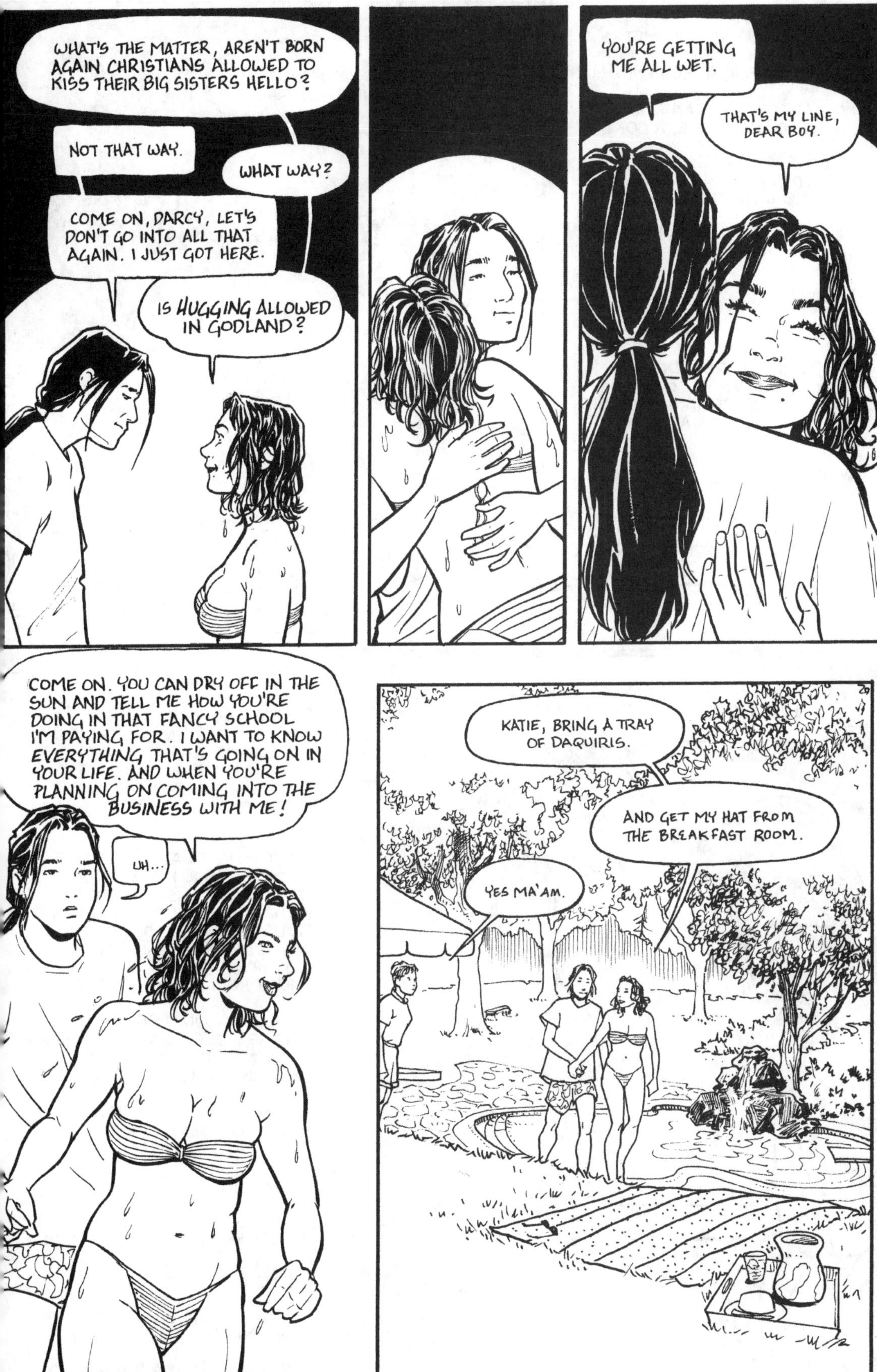
WHAT'S THE MATTER, AREN'T BORN AGAIN CHRISTIANS ALLOWED TO KISS THEIR BIG SISTERS HELLO?
NOT THAT WAY.
WHAT WAY?
COME ON, DARCY, LET'S DON'T GO INTO ALL THAT AGAIN. I JUST GOT HERE.
IS HUGGING ALLOWED IN GODLAND?
YOU'RE GETTING ME ALL WET.
THAT'S MY LINE, DEAR BOY.
COME ON. YOU CAN DRY OFF IN THE SUN AND TELL ME HOW YOU'RE DOING IN THAT FANCY SCHOOL I'M PAYING FOR. I WANT TO KNOW EVERYTHING THAT'S GOING ON IN YOUR LIFE. AND WHEN YOU'RE PLANNING ON COMING INTO THE BUSINESS WITH ME!
UH...
KATIE, BRING A TRAY OF DAQUIRIS.
AND GET MY HAT FROM THE BREAKFAST ROOM.
YES MA'AM.

DAVID, DO YOU WANT SOMETHING TO EAT? YOU MUST BE HUNGRY AFTER THE FLIGHT FROM NEW YORK.

NO, I ATE ON THE PLANE. THANKS. OH, DO YOU HAVE LIKE, A COKE?

OF COURSE. **KATIE, BRING ME THE IVORY BOX IN MY DESK. THE ONE WITH THE...**

I MEAN A COCA-COLA, DARCY. .... LIKE YOU *DRINK*?

OH. ...NEVER MIND, KATIE. JUST A SOFT DRINK FOR THE BOY.

YES MA'AM.

GOOD GRIEF, DARCY. DO YOU *REALLY* THINK I'M GOING TO WALK IN AND DEMAND **COCAINE** TO SNORT ON THE BACK LAWN?

YOU CAN HAVE WHATEVER YOU LIKE HERE, 'SAKA. THIS IS YOUR HOUSE, TOO. AND THANKS TO MY SOON TO BE LATE GREAT HUSBAND, WE HAVE MORE MONEY THAN *GOD*!

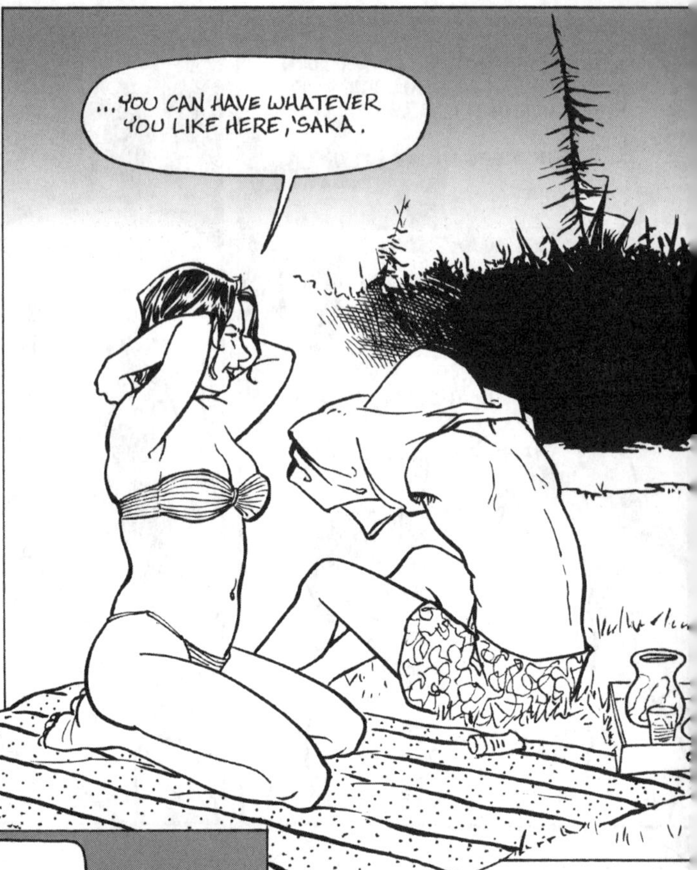
...YOU CAN HAVE WHATEVER YOU LIKE HERE, 'SAKA.

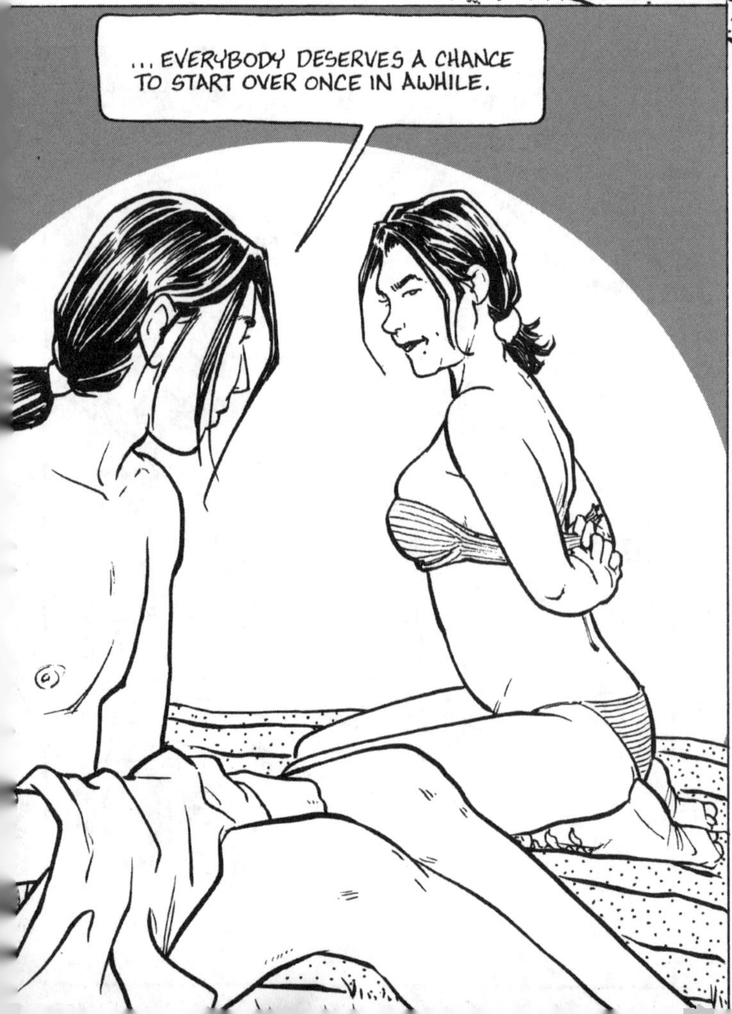
... EVERYBODY DESERVES A CHANCE TO START OVER ONCE IN AWHILE.

DARCY, I DON'T DO DRUGS. AND PLEASE DON'T REFER TO ME BY THAT NAME AGAIN. YOUSAKA TAKAHASHI IS A PAST I WANT TO LEAVE BEHIND. MY NAME IS DAVID QIN.

NO IT ISN'T. THAT'S THE NAME OF THE BOY YOU KILLED THREE YEARS AGO. I WISH TO HELL YOU'D GROW OUT OF THIS WHOLE PIOUS GUILT TRIP OF DEDICATING YOUR LIFE TO HIS HONOR. IT'S SUCH A CORNBALL CLICHÉ AND IT REALLY PISSES ME OFF.

WOULD YOU JUST DO IT FOR ME, PLEASE? EVERYBODY DESERVES A CHANCE TO START OVER ONCE IN AWHILE.

OH, ALL RIGHT. YOU WERE A LOT MORE FUN BEFORE YOU FOUND RELIGION... ***DAVID!***

THANK YOU.

SIGH WHAT A WASTE. I HAD SUCH PLANS FOR THE THREE OF US.

THREE OF US?

YOU... AND ME... AND THE TANNING OIL.

DARCY, YOU NEED A BOYFRIEND.

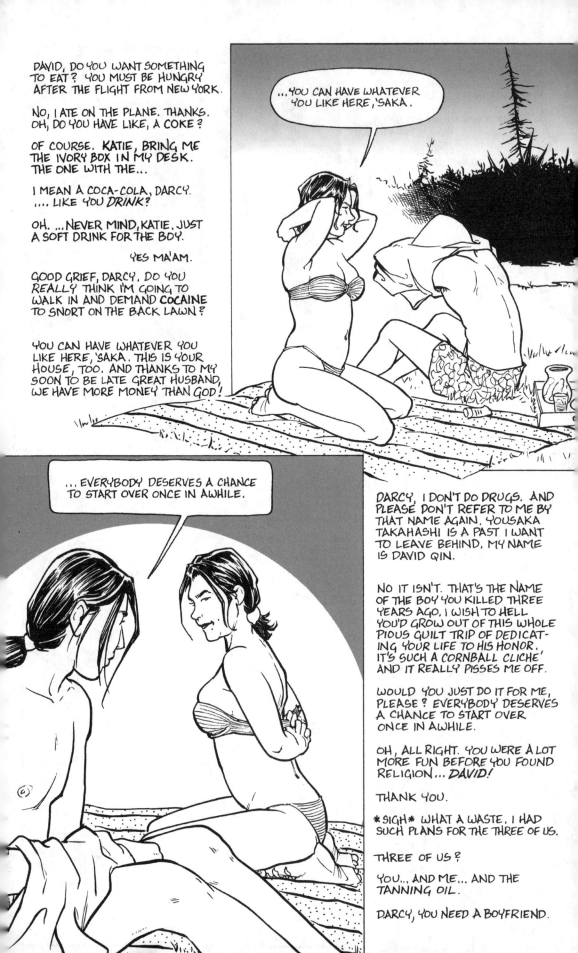

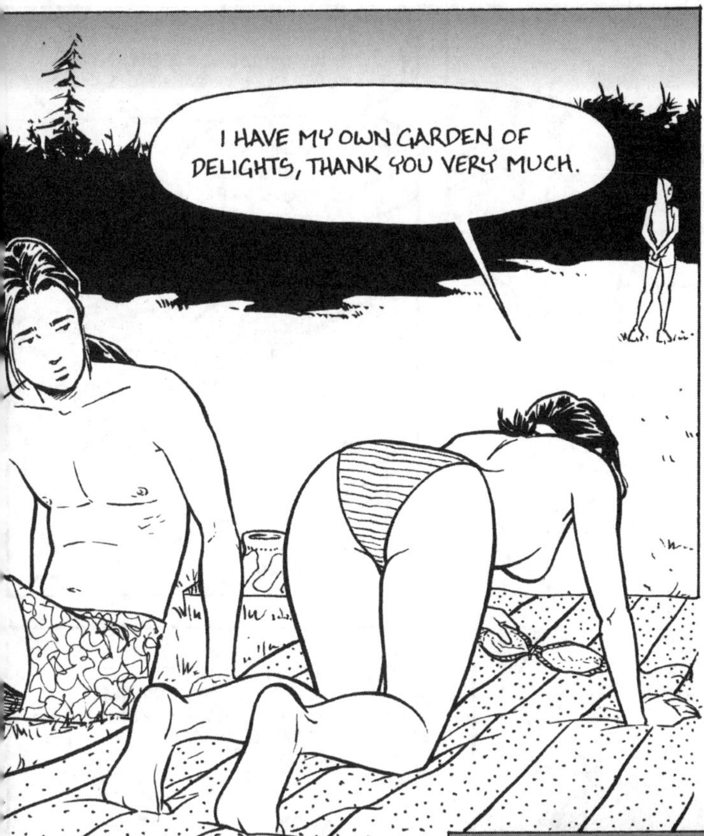
I HAVE MY OWN GARDEN OF DELIGHTS, THANK YOU VERY MUCH.

BOYFRIENDS ARE FOR SCHOOLGIRLS, LITTLE BROTHER. I HAVE MY OWN GARDEN OF DELIGHTS, THANK YOU VERY MUCH.

DO YOU EVER SEE MITCHELL?

WHO?

MITCHELL PARKER. YOUR *HUSBAND*?

UGH! THAT BAG OF BONES? GOD **NO!** I WON'T LET HIM COME **NEAR** ME. HE STAYS IN D.C. AND I STAY HERE IN L.A., WAITING FOR THE OLD FART TO CHEAT ON ME OR DIE... EITHER WAY, I DON'T CARE.

WHY DID YOU MARRY HIM IF YOU DON'T WANT TO BE AROUND HIM?

BECAUSE WE NEEDED THE **MONEY!** YOU DON'T KNOW ABOUT THINGS LIKE THAT BECAUSE I SHIELD YOU FROM THEM, BUT WE HAD SERIOUS FINANCIAL TROUBLES AFTER FATHER WAS MURDERED.

YOU NEVER TOLD ME THAT.

LIKE I SAID, I SHIELD YOU.

THE FRIKKIN' YAKUZA SHUT US OUT AND TRIED TO TAKE AWAY EVERYTHING HE WORKED FOR. IF I HADN'T TAKEN OVER AND GONE INTO BUSINESS WITH THE AMERICANS, I DON'T KNOW WHAT WE WOULD HAVE DONE. *COUGH! COUGH!*

GET A JOB, LIKE EVERYONE ELSE.

YOU'VE GOT TO BE KIDDING.

JUST A SUGGESTION.

DRINK YOUR SODA POP, CHOIR BOY.

(LONG MINUTES PASS BEFORE DARCY SPEAKS AGAIN.)

I'M THROWING A PARTY TOMORROW NIGHT. DO YOU WANT ME TO GET YOU A DATE? I KNOW HUNDREDS OF YOUNG MODELS WHO WOULD LOVE TO BE SEEN ON THE ARM OF A RICH YOUNG STUD.

NO, DARCY. NO. I'M NOT DOING ANYTHING WITH YOUR "MODELS".

DON'T BE A WALLFLOWER, DAVID.

HEY, YOU CALLED ME *DAVID!*

YEAH, SEE? NOW YOU OWE ME.

OH MAN.

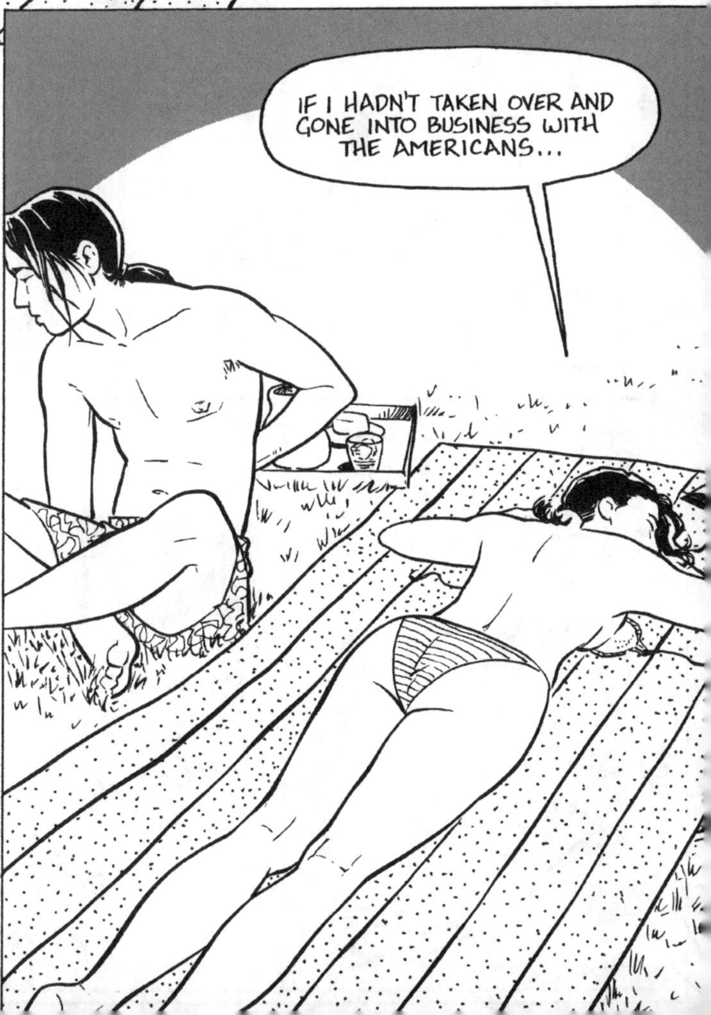
IF I HADN'T TAKEN OVER AND GONE INTO BUSINESS WITH THE AMERICANS...

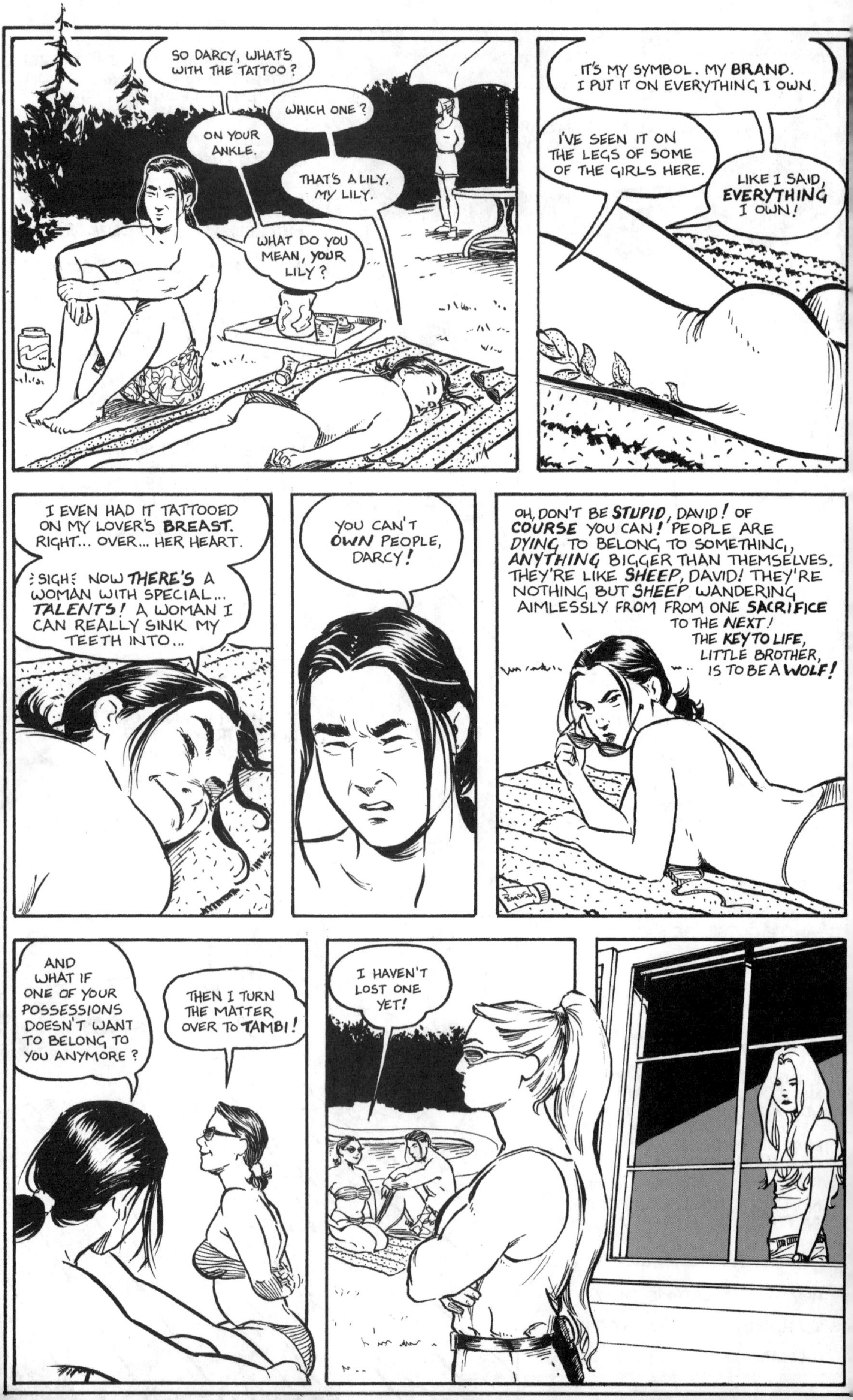
SO DARCY, WHAT'S WITH THE TATTOO?
WHICH ONE?
ON YOUR ANKLE.
THAT'S A LILY. MY LILY.
WHAT DO YOU MEAN, YOUR LILY?
IT'S MY SYMBOL. MY BRAND. I PUT IT ON EVERYTHING I OWN.
I'VE SEEN IT ON THE LEGS OF SOME OF THE GIRLS HERE.
LIKE I SAID, EVERYTHING I OWN!
I EVEN HAD IT TATTOOED ON MY LOVER'S BREAST. RIGHT... OVER... HER HEART.
SIGH NOW THERE'S A WOMAN WITH SPECIAL... TALENTS! A WOMAN I CAN REALLY SINK MY TEETH INTO...
YOU CAN'T OWN PEOPLE, DARCY!
OH, DON'T BE STUPID, DAVID! OF COURSE YOU CAN! PEOPLE ARE DYING TO BELONG TO SOMETHING, ANYTHING BIGGER THAN THEMSELVES. THEY'RE LIKE SHEEP, DAVID! THEY'RE NOTHING BUT SHEEP WANDERING AIMLESSLY FROM FROM ONE SACRIFICE TO THE NEXT! THE KEY TO LIFE, LITTLE BROTHER, IS TO BE A WOLF!
AND WHAT IF ONE OF YOUR POSSESSIONS DOESN'T WANT TO BELONG TO YOU ANYMORE?
THEN I TURN THE MATTER OVER TO TAMBI!
I HAVEN'T LOST ONE YET!

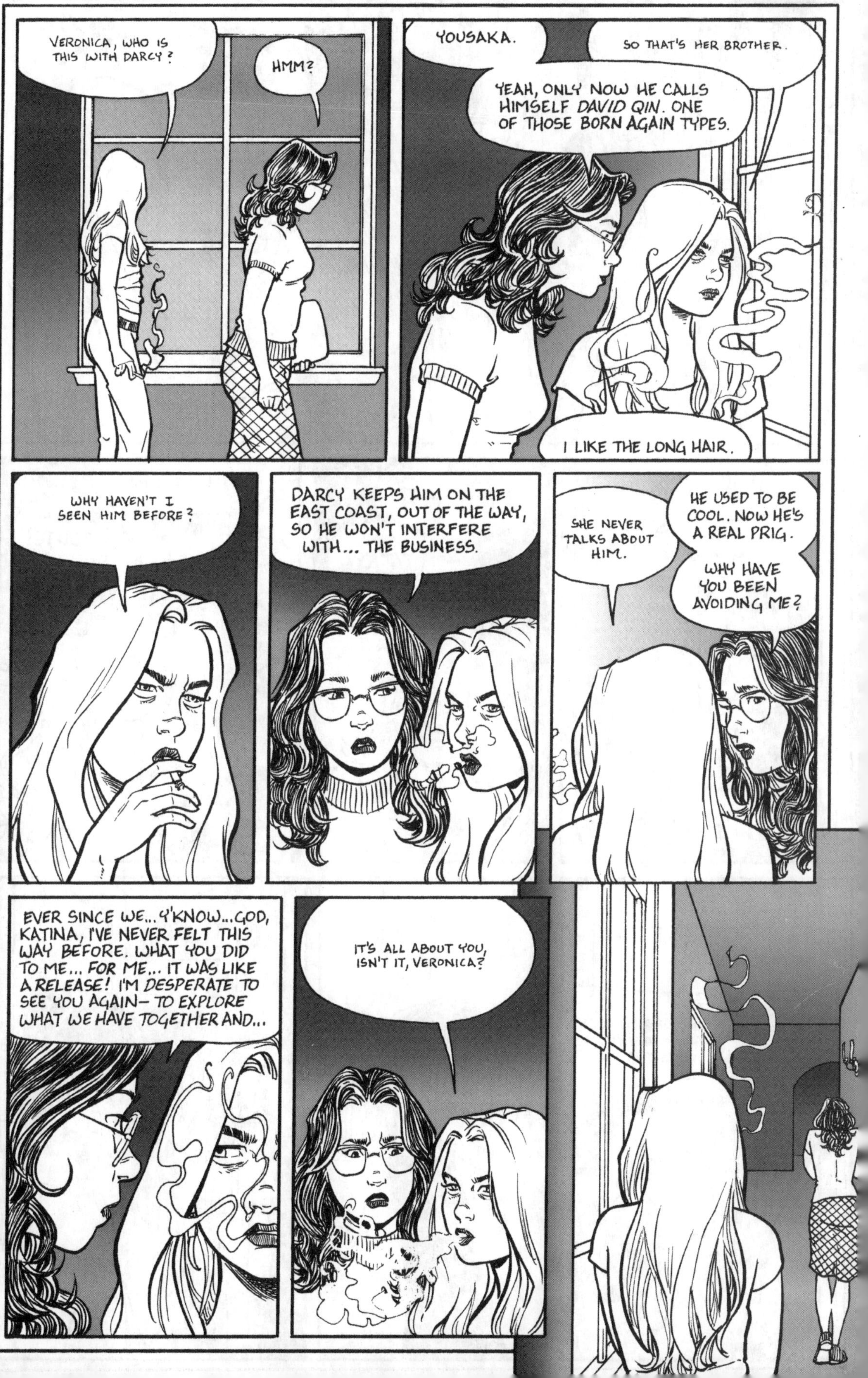
VERONICA, WHO IS THIS WITH DARCY?
HMM?
YOUSAKA.
SO THAT'S HER BROTHER.
YEAH, ONLY NOW HE CALLS HIMSELF DAVID QIN. ONE OF THOSE BORN AGAIN TYPES.
I LIKE THE LONG HAIR.
WHY HAVEN'T I SEEN HIM BEFORE?
DARCY KEEPS HIM ON THE EAST COAST, OUT OF THE WAY, SO HE WON'T INTERFERE WITH... THE BUSINESS.
SHE NEVER TALKS ABOUT HIM.
HE USED TO BE COOL. NOW HE'S A REAL PRIG.
WHY HAVE YOU BEEN AVOIDING ME?
EVER SINCE WE... Y'KNOW... GOD, KATINA, I'VE NEVER FELT THIS WAY BEFORE. WHAT YOU DID TO ME... FOR ME... IT WAS LIKE A RELEASE! I'M DESPERATE TO SEE YOU AGAIN– TO EXPLORE WHAT WE HAVE TOGETHER AND...
IT'S ALL ABOUT YOU, ISN'T IT, VERONICA?

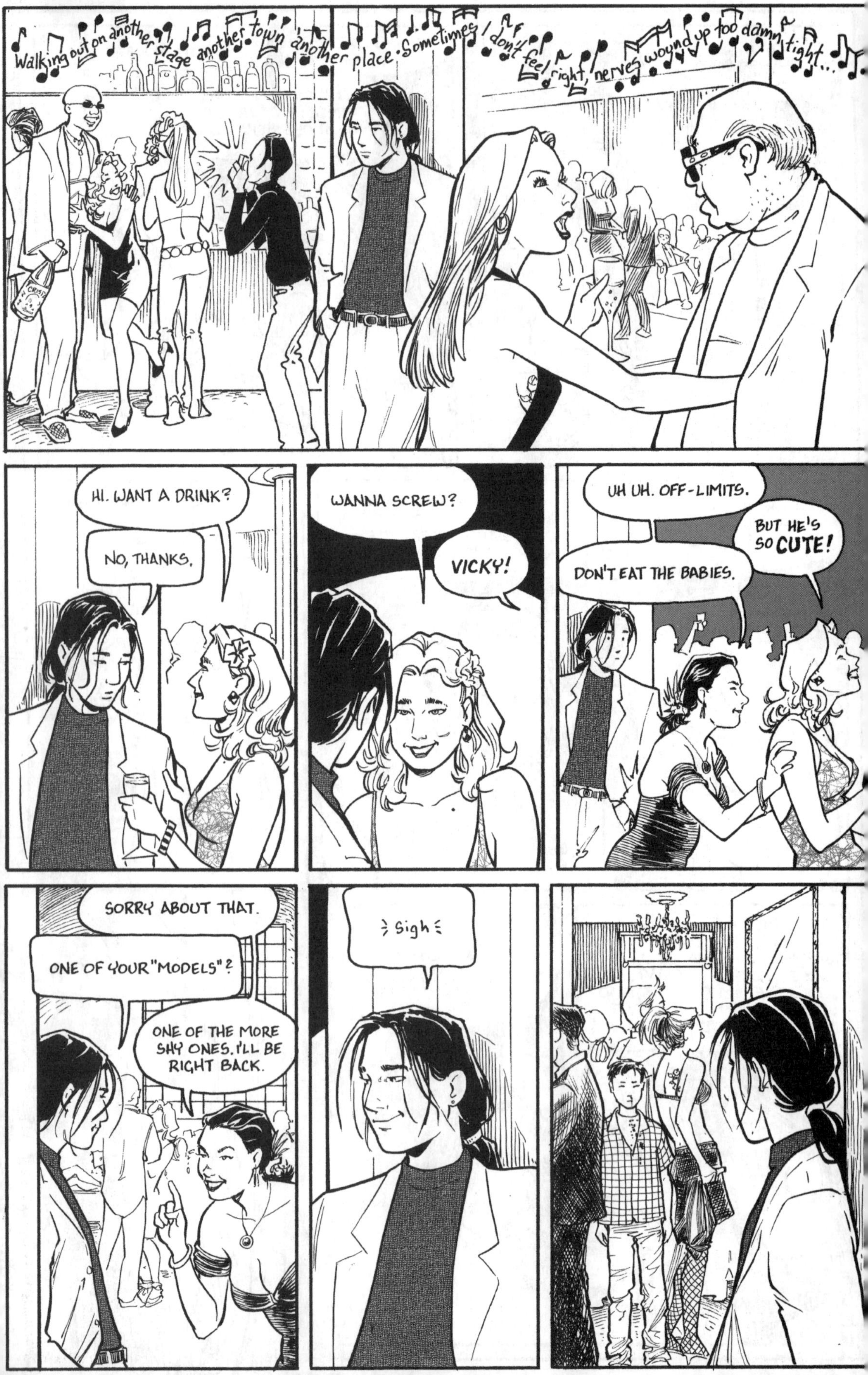
Walking out on another stage another town another place. Sometimes I don't feel right, nerves wound up too damn tight...
HI. WANT A DRINK?
NO, THANKS.
WANNA SCREW?
VICKY!
UH UH. OFF-LIMITS.
DON'T EAT THE BABIES.
BUT HE'S SO CUTE!
SORRY ABOUT THAT.
ONE OF YOUR "MODELS"?
ONE OF THE MORE SHY ONES. I'LL BE RIGHT BACK.
sigh

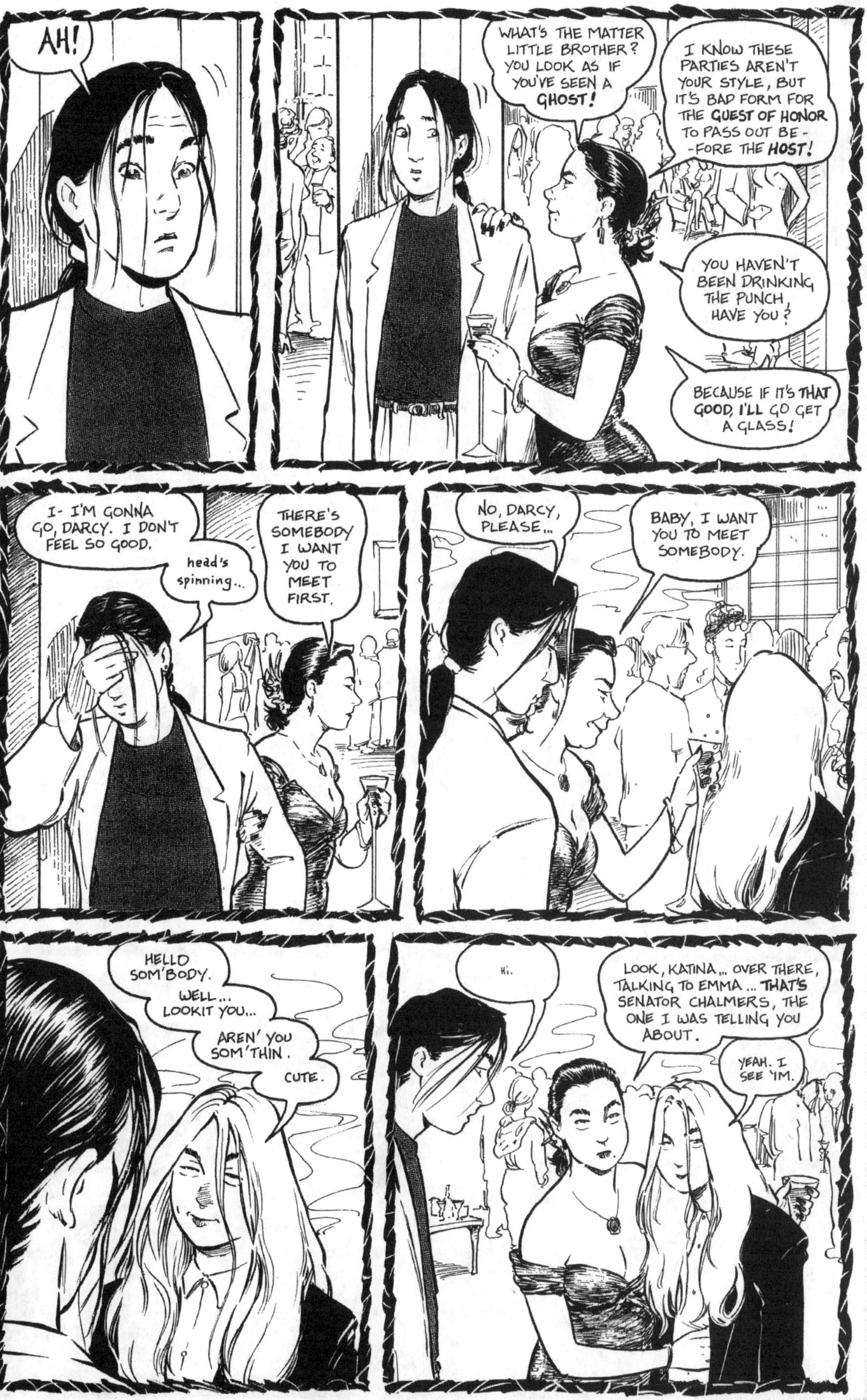
AH!
WHAT'S THE MATTER LITTLE BROTHER? YOU LOOK AS IF YOU'VE SEEN A GHOST!
I KNOW THESE PARTIES AREN'T YOUR STYLE, BUT IT'S BAD FORM FOR THE GUEST OF HONOR TO PASS OUT BE- -FORE THE HOST!
YOU HAVEN'T BEEN DRINKING THE PUNCH, HAVE YOU?
BECAUSE IF IT'S THAT GOOD, I'LL GO GET A GLASS!
I- I'M GONNA GO, DARCY. I DON'T FEEL SO GOOD.
head's spinning...
THERE'S SOMEBODY I WANT YOU TO MEET FIRST.
NO, DARCY, PLEASE...
BABY, I WANT YOU TO MEET SOMEBODY.
HELLO SOM'BODY.
WELL... LOOKIT YOU...
AREN' YOU SOM'THIN.
CUTE.
Hi.
LOOK, KATINA... OVER THERE, TALKING TO EMMA... THAT'S SENATOR CHALMERS, THE ONE I WAS TELLING YOU ABOUT.
YEAH. I SEE 'YM.

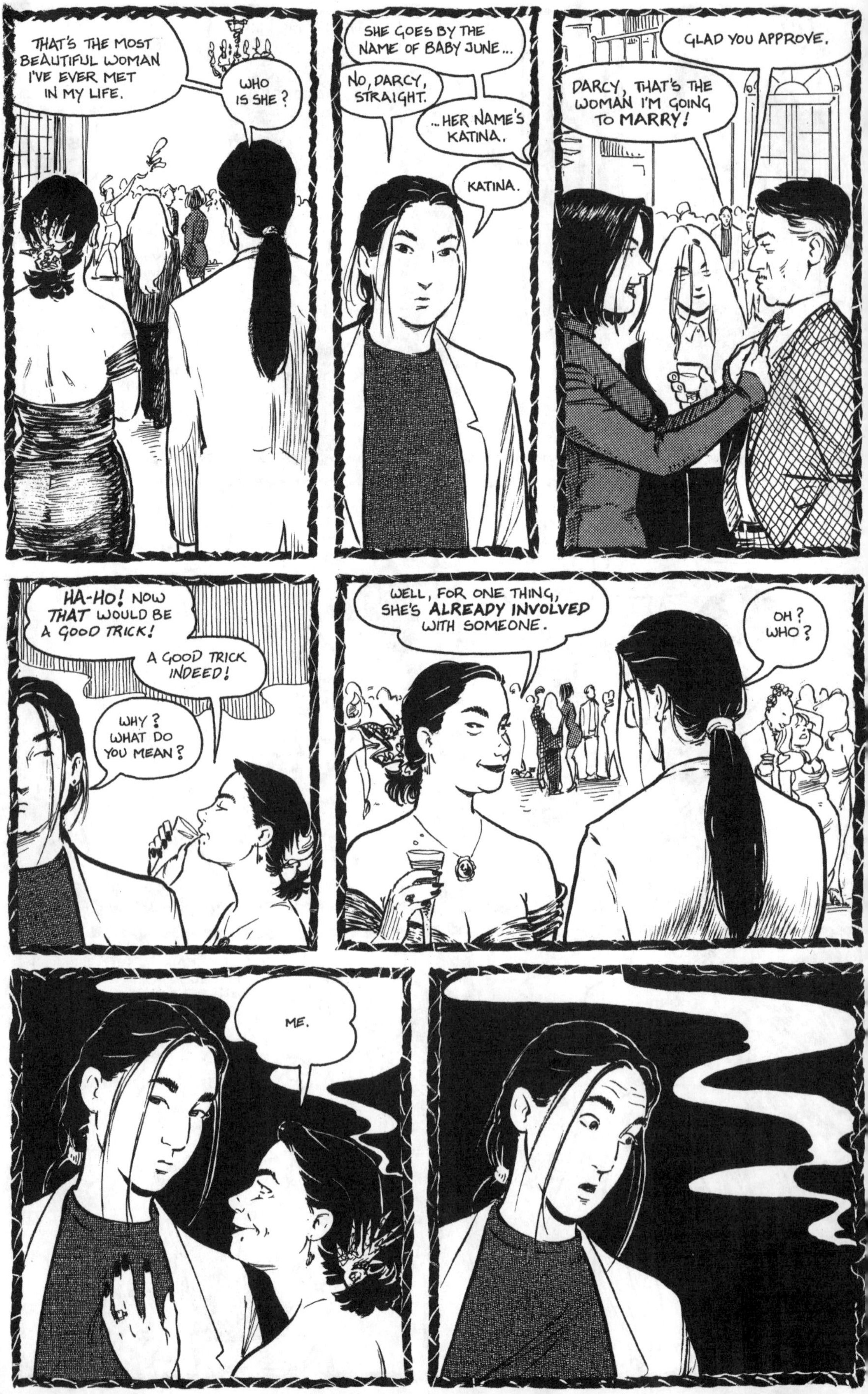

THAT'S THE MOST BEAUTIFUL WOMAN I'VE EVER MET IN MY LIFE.
WHO IS SHE?
SHE GOES BY THE NAME OF BABY JUNE...
NO, DARCY, STRAIGHT.
...HER NAME'S KATINA.
KATINA.
GLAD YOU APPROVE.
DARCY, THAT'S THE WOMAN I'M GOING TO MARRY!
HA-HO! NOW THAT WOULD BE A GOOD TRICK!
A GOOD TRICK INDEED!
WHY? WHAT DO YOU MEAN?
WELL, FOR ONE THING, SHE'S ALREADY INVOLVED WITH SOMEONE.
OH? WHO?
ME.

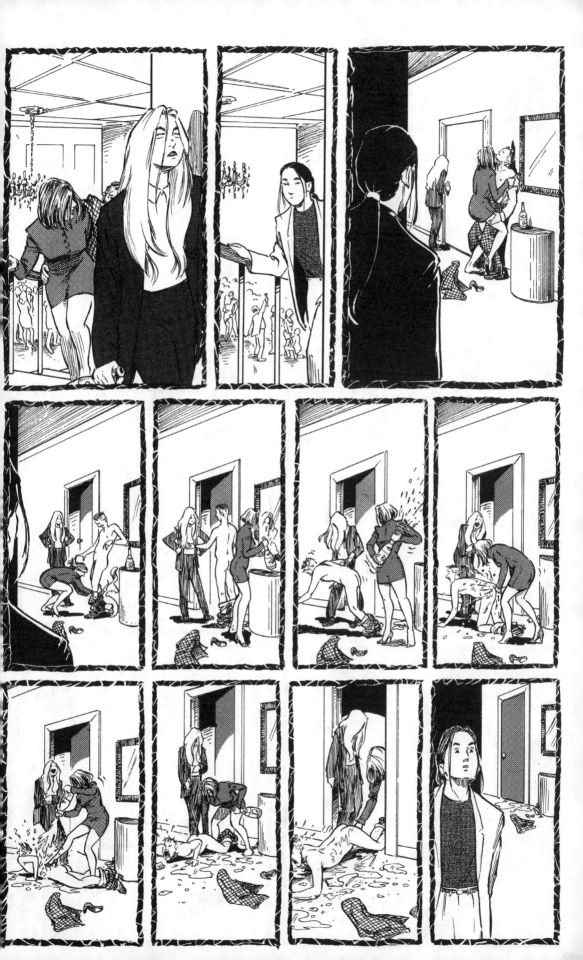

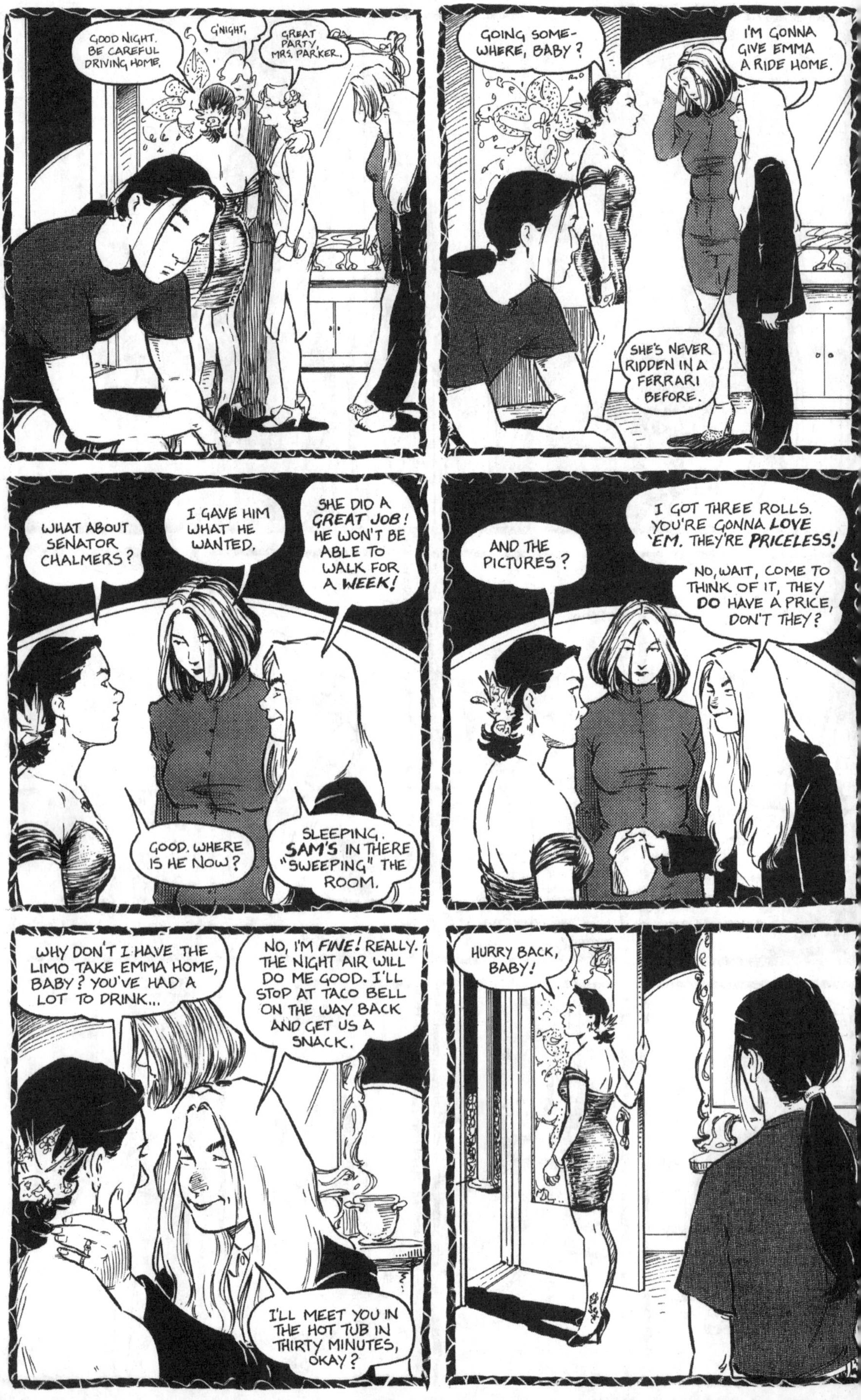
GOOD NIGHT. BE CAREFUL DRIVING HOME.
G'NIGHT.
GREAT PARTY, MRS. PARKER.
GOING SOME-WHERE, BABY?
I'M GONNA GIVE EMMA A RIDE HOME.
SHE'S NEVER RIDDEN IN A FERRARI BEFORE.
WHAT ABOUT SENATOR CHALMERS?
I GAVE HIM WHAT HE WANTED.
SHE DID A GREAT JOB! HE WON'T BE ABLE TO WALK FOR A WEEK!
GOOD. WHERE IS HE NOW?
SLEEPING. SAM'S IN THERE "SWEEPING" THE ROOM.
AND THE PICTURES?
I GOT THREE ROLLS. YOU'RE GONNA LOVE 'EM. THEY'RE PRICELESS!
NO, WAIT, COME TO THINK OF IT, THEY DO HAVE A PRICE, DON'T THEY?
WHY DON'T I HAVE THE LIMO TAKE EMMA HOME, BABY? YOU'VE HAD A LOT TO DRINK...
NO, I'M FINE! REALLY. THE NIGHT AIR WILL DO ME GOOD. I'LL STOP AT TACO BELL ON THE WAY BACK AND GET US A SNACK.
I'LL MEET YOU IN THE HOT TUB IN THIRTY MINUTES, OKAY?
HURRY BACK, BABY!

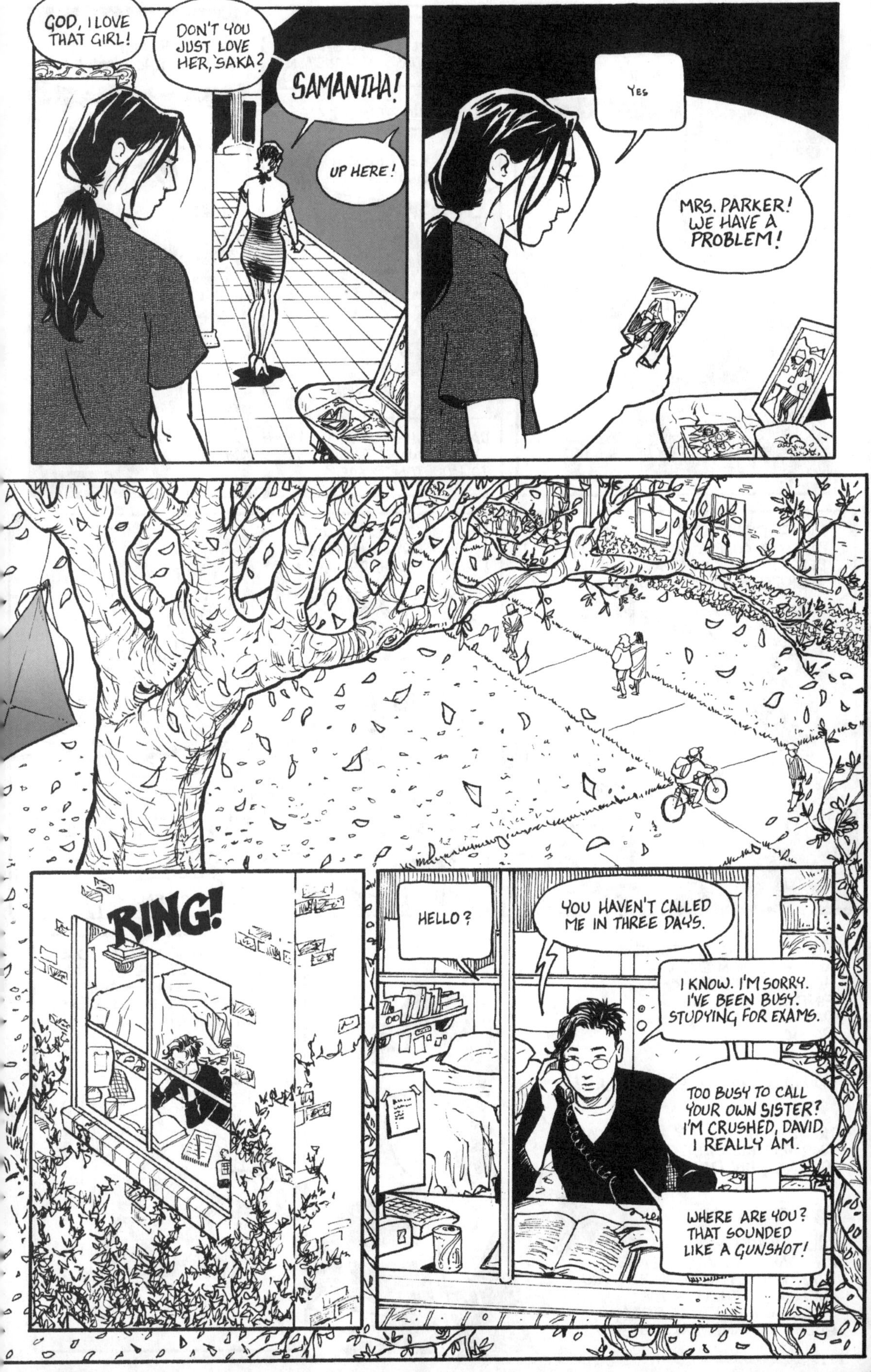
GOD, I LOVE THAT GIRL!
DON'T YOU JUST LOVE HER, 'SAKA?
SAMANTHA!
UP HERE!
YES
MRS. PARKER! WE HAVE A PROBLEM!
RING!
HELLO?
YOU HAVEN'T CALLED ME IN THREE DAYS.
I KNOW. I'M SORRY. I'VE BEEN BUSY. STUDYING FOR EXAMS.
TOO BUSY TO CALL YOUR OWN SISTER? I'M CRUSHED, DAVID. I REALLY AM.
WHERE ARE YOU? THAT SOUNDED LIKE A GUNSHOT!

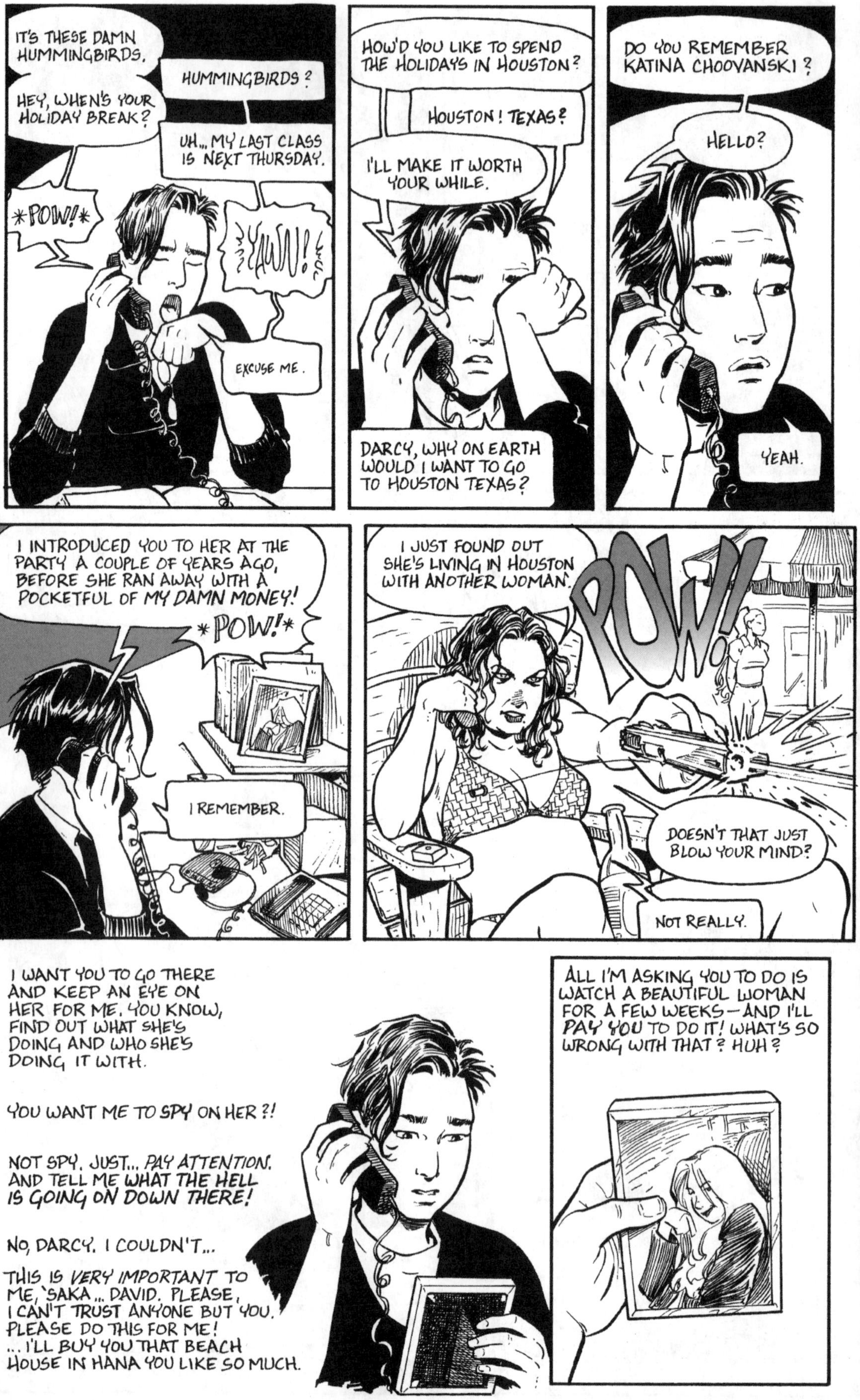

IT'S THESE DAMN HUMMINGBIRDS.
HUMMINGBIRDS?
HEY, WHEN'S YOUR HOLIDAY BREAK?
UH... MY LAST CLASS IS NEXT THURSDAY.
POW!
YAWN!
EXCUSE ME.
HOW'D YOU LIKE TO SPEND THE HOLIDAYS IN HOUSTON?
HOUSTON! TEXAS?
I'LL MAKE IT WORTH YOUR WHILE.
DARCY, WHY ON EARTH WOULD I WANT TO GO TO HOUSTON TEXAS?
DO YOU REMEMBER KATINA CHOOVANSKI?
HELLO?
YEAH.
I INTRODUCED YOU TO HER AT THE PARTY A COUPLE OF YEARS AGO, BEFORE SHE RAN AWAY WITH A POCKETFUL OF MY DAMN MONEY!
POW!
I REMEMBER.
I JUST FOUND OUT SHE'S LIVING IN HOUSTON WITH ANOTHER WOMAN.
POW!!
DOESN'T THAT JUST BLOW YOUR MIND?
NOT REALLY.
I WANT YOU TO GO THERE AND KEEP AN EYE ON HER FOR ME. YOU KNOW, FIND OUT WHAT SHE'S DOING AND WHO SHE'S DOING IT WITH.
YOU WANT ME TO SPY ON HER?!
NOT SPY. JUST... PAY ATTENTION. AND TELL ME WHAT THE HELL IS GOING ON DOWN THERE!
NO, DARCY. I COULDN'T...
THIS IS VERY IMPORTANT TO ME, 'SAKA... DAVID. PLEASE, I CAN'T TRUST ANYONE BUT YOU. PLEASE DO THIS FOR ME! ... I'LL BUY YOU THAT BEACH HOUSE IN HANA YOU LIKE SO MUCH.
ALL I'M ASKING YOU TO DO IS WATCH A BEAUTIFUL WOMAN FOR A FEW WEEKS—AND I'LL PAY YOU TO DO IT! WHAT'S SO WRONG WITH THAT? HUH?

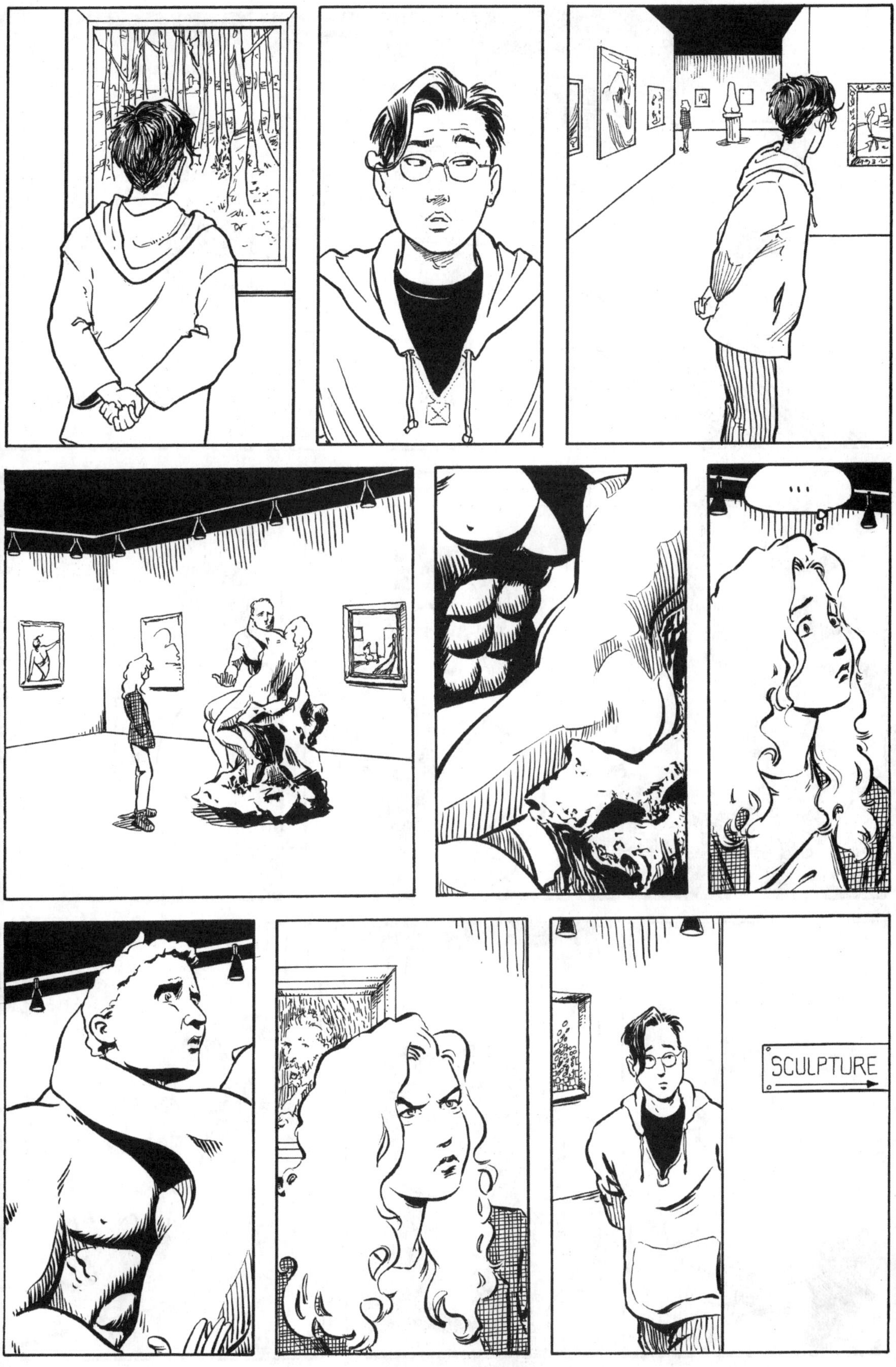
...
SCULPTURE

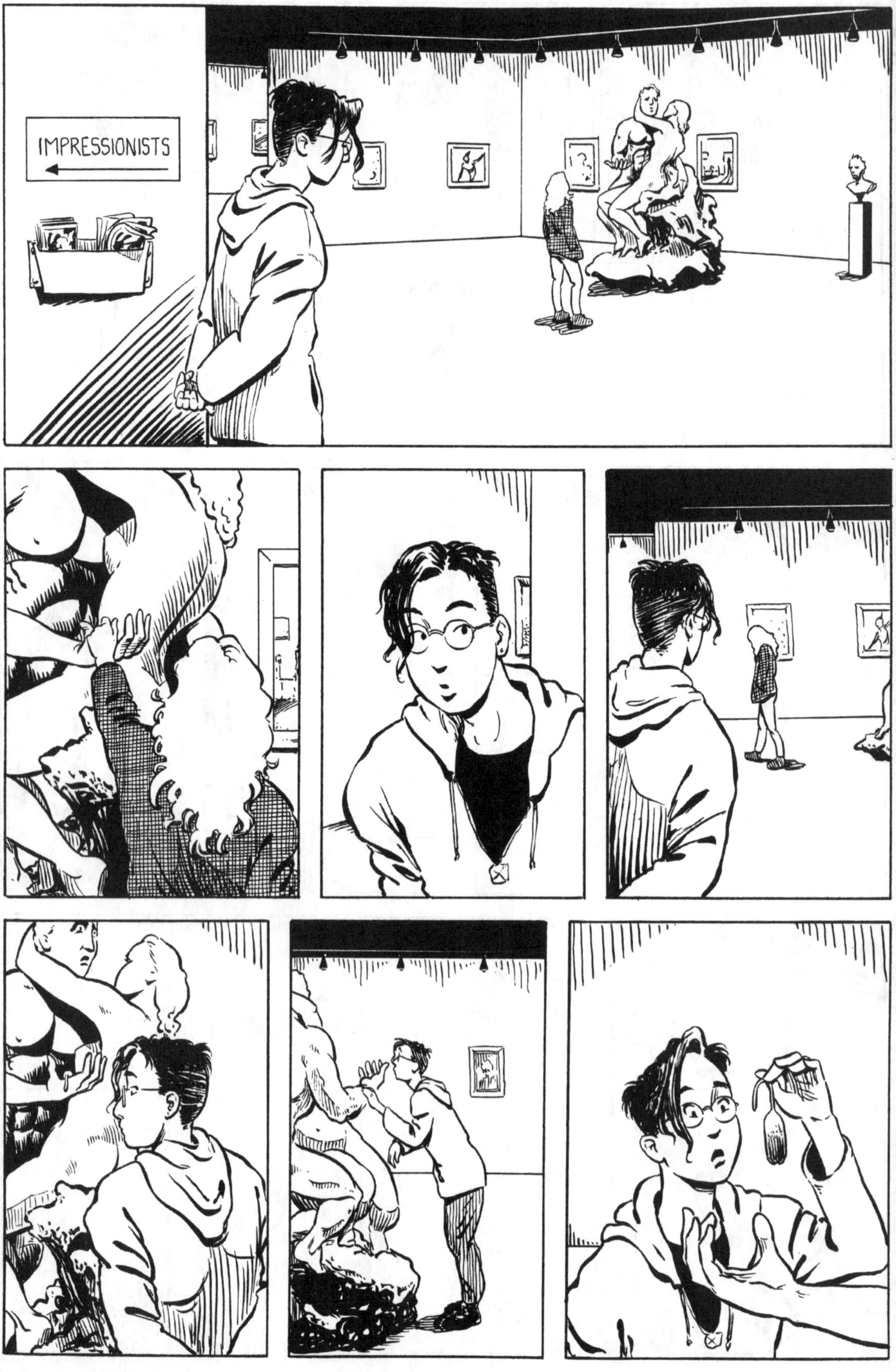
IMPRESSIONISTS

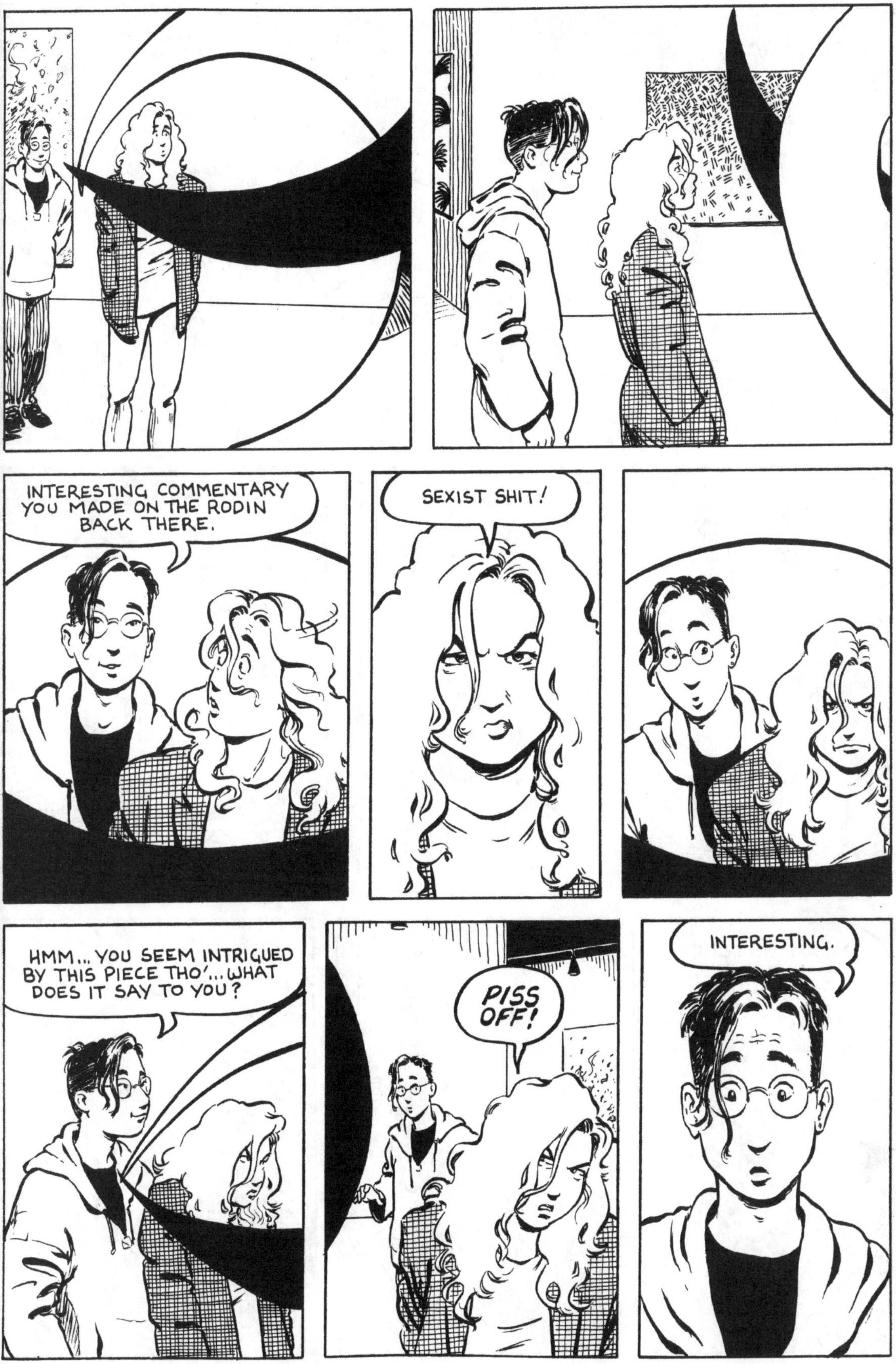
INTERESTING COMMENTARY YOU MADE ON THE RODIN BACK THERE.
SEXIST SHIT!
HMM... YOU SEEM INTRIGUED BY THIS PIECE THO'... WHAT DOES IT SAY TO YOU?
PISS OFF!
INTERESTING.

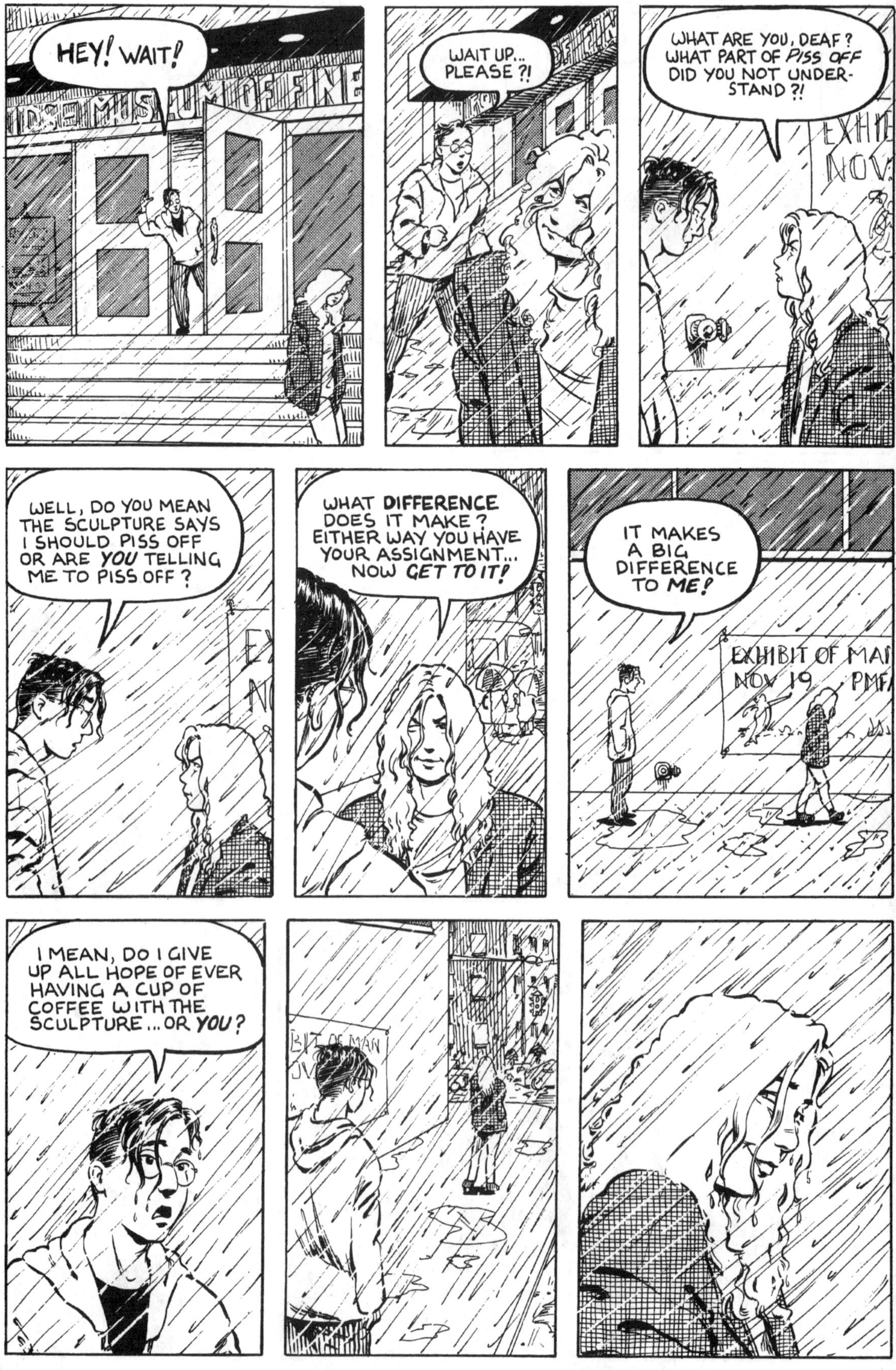

HEY! WAIT!
WAIT UP... PLEASE?!
WHAT ARE YOU, DEAF? WHAT PART OF PISS OFF DID YOU NOT UNDER-STAND?!
WELL, DO YOU MEAN THE SCULPTURE SAYS I SHOULD PISS OFF OR ARE YOU TELLING ME TO PISS OFF?
WHAT DIFFERENCE DOES IT MAKE? EITHER WAY YOU HAVE YOUR ASSIGNMENT... NOW GET TO IT!
IT MAKES A BIG DIFFERENCE TO ME!
EXHIBIT OF MAN
NOV 19
I MEAN, DO I GIVE UP ALL HOPE OF EVER HAVING A CUP OF COFFEE WITH THE SCULPTURE... OR YOU?

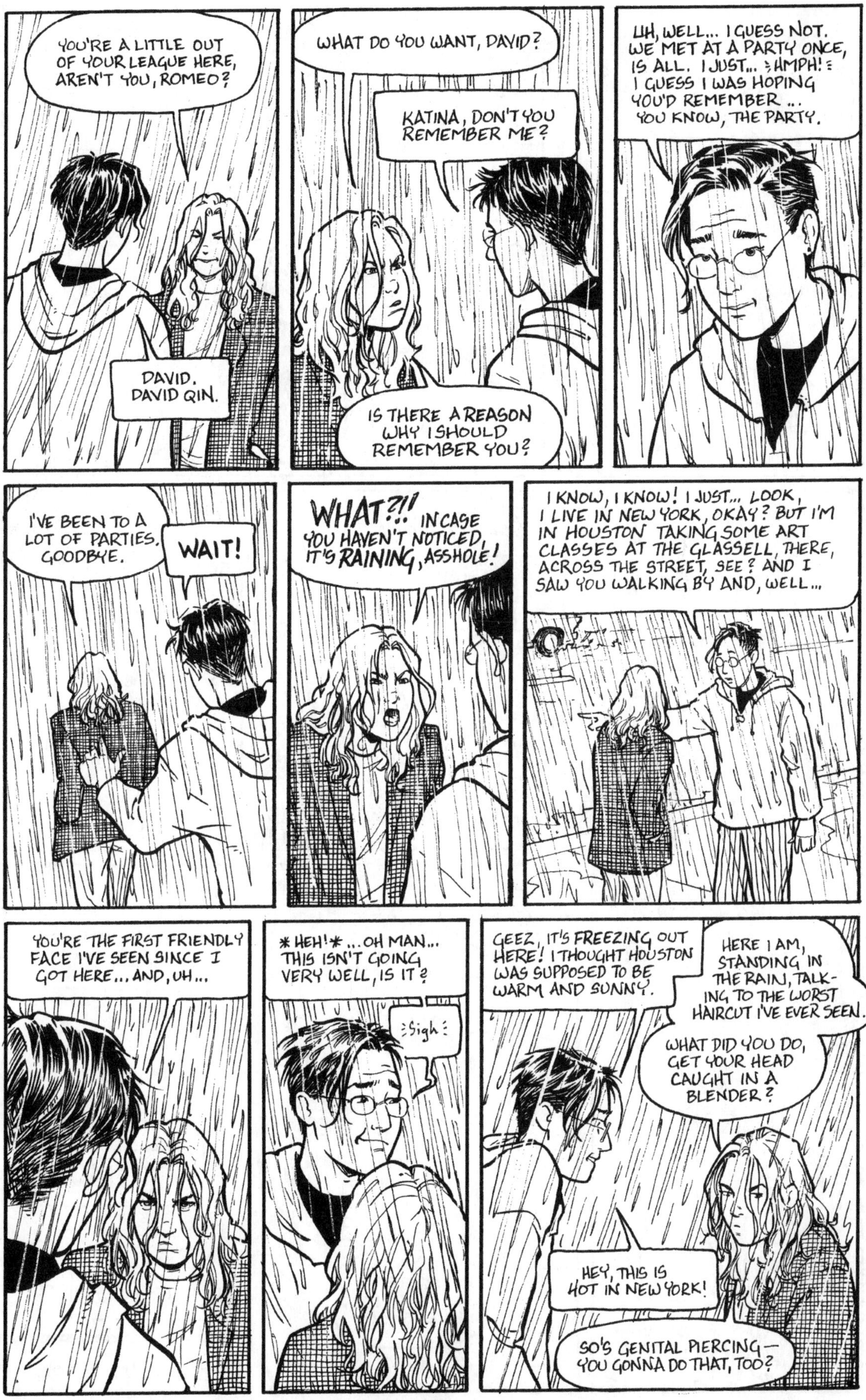
YOU'RE A LITTLE OUT OF YOUR LEAGUE HERE, AREN'T YOU, ROMEO?
DAVID. DAVID QIN.
WHAT DO YOU WANT, DAVID?
KATINA, DON'T YOU REMEMBER ME?
IS THERE A REASON WHY I SHOULD REMEMBER YOU?
UH, WELL... I GUESS NOT. WE MET AT A PARTY ONCE, IS ALL. I JUST... HMPH! I GUESS I WAS HOPING YOU'D REMEMBER ... YOU KNOW, THE PARTY.
I'VE BEEN TO A LOT OF PARTIES. GOODBYE.
WAIT!
WHAT?!! IN CASE YOU HAVEN'T NOTICED, IT'S RAINING, ASSHOLE!
I KNOW, I KNOW! I JUST... LOOK, I LIVE IN NEW YORK, OKAY? BUT I'M IN HOUSTON TAKING SOME ART CLASSES AT THE GLASSELL, THERE, ACROSS THE STREET, SEE? AND I SAW YOU WALKING BY AND, WELL...
YOU'RE THE FIRST FRIENDLY FACE I'VE SEEN SINCE I GOT HERE... AND, UH...
HEH! ...OH MAN... THIS ISN'T GOING VERY WELL, IS IT?
Sigh
GEEZ, IT'S FREEZING OUT HERE! I THOUGHT HOUSTON WAS SUPPOSED TO BE WARM AND SUNNY.
HERE I AM, STANDING IN THE RAIN, TALKING TO THE WORST HAIRCUT I'VE EVER SEEN.
WHAT DID YOU DO, GET YOUR HEAD CAUGHT IN A BLENDER?
HEY, THIS IS HOT IN NEW YORK!
SO'S GENITAL PIERCING— YOU GONNA DO THAT, TOO?

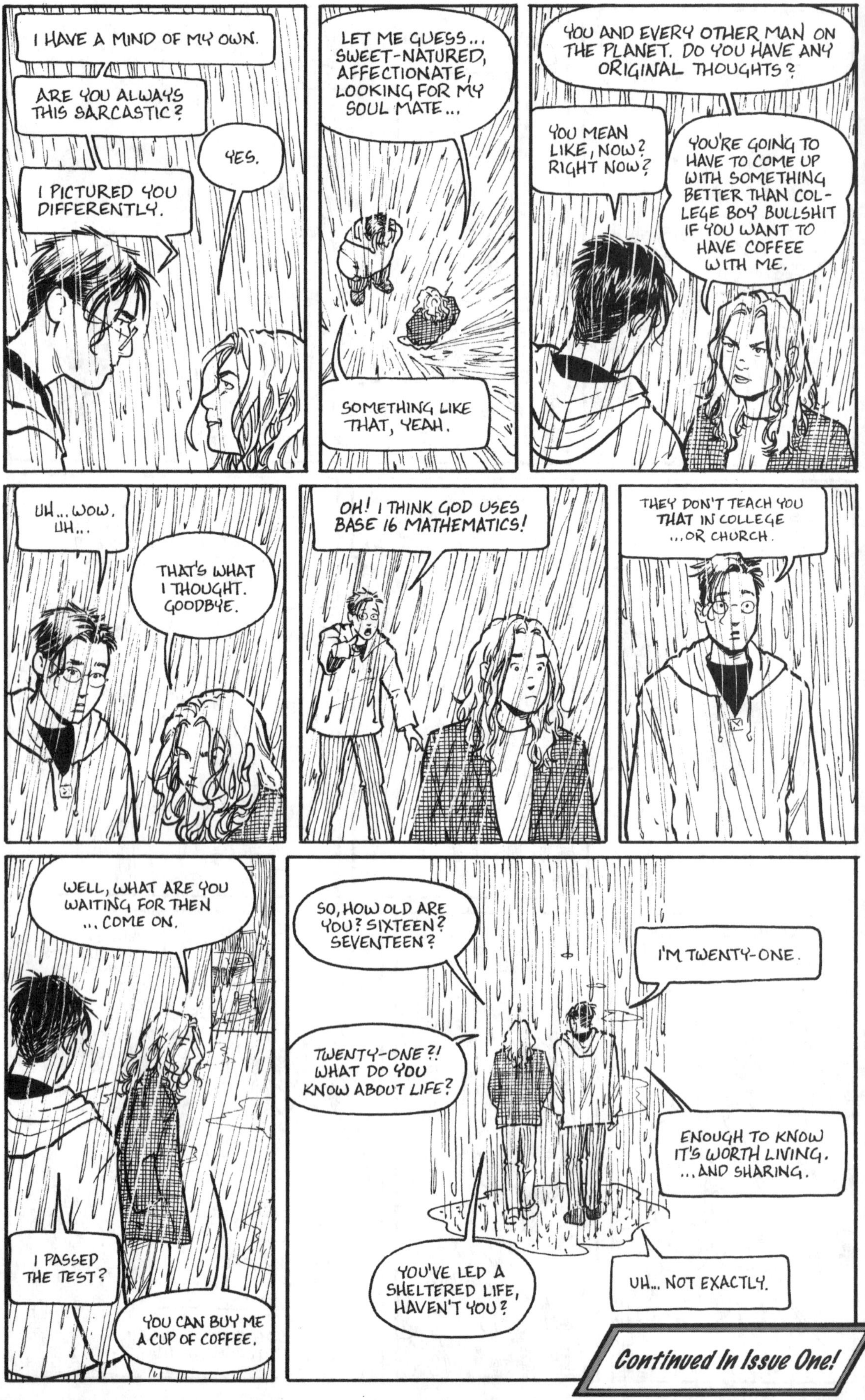
I HAVE A MIND OF MY OWN.
ARE YOU ALWAYS THIS SARCASTIC?
YES.
I PICTURED YOU DIFFERENTLY.
LET ME GUESS... SWEET-NATURED, AFFECTIONATE, LOOKING FOR MY SOUL MATE...
SOMETHING LIKE THAT, YEAH.
YOU AND EVERY OTHER MAN ON THE PLANET. DO YOU HAVE ANY ORIGINAL THOUGHTS?
YOU MEAN LIKE, NOW? RIGHT NOW?
YOU'RE GOING TO HAVE TO COME UP WITH SOMETHING BETTER THAN COL-LEGE BOY BULLSHIT IF YOU WANT TO HAVE COFFEE WITH ME.
UH... WOW. UH...
THAT'S WHAT I THOUGHT. GOODBYE.
OH! I THINK GOD USES BASE 16 MATHEMATICS!
THEY DON'T TEACH YOU THAT IN COLLEGE ...OR CHURCH.
WELL, WHAT ARE YOU WAITING FOR THEN ... COME ON.
I PASSED THE TEST?
YOU CAN BUY ME A CUP OF COFFEE.
SO, HOW OLD ARE YOU? SIXTEEN? SEVENTEEN?
I'M TWENTY-ONE.
TWENTY-ONE?! WHAT DO YOU KNOW ABOUT LIFE?
ENOUGH TO KNOW IT'S WORTH LIVING. ...AND SHARING.
YOU'VE LED A SHELTERED LIFE, HAVEN'T YOU?
UH... NOT EXACTLY.

Continued In Issue One!

The David

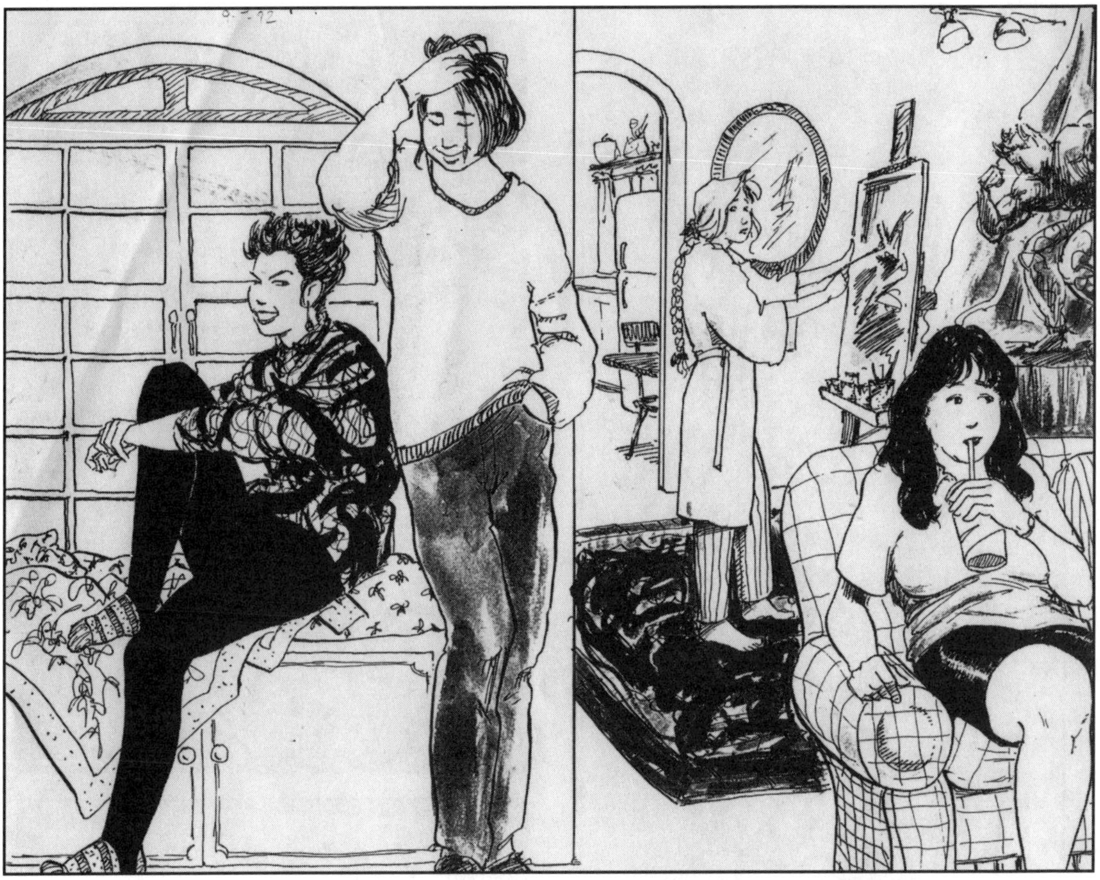

My David

Our hero comes from a long line of David's...King David, Michelangelo's David, Davey Jones of The Monkees...all great patriarchs to the young man who brings a soulful voice to SiP.

David began as a comic strip character, a laid back cool cat with an understated insight into love with a pretty girl who wouldn't give him the time of day.

Sound familiar?

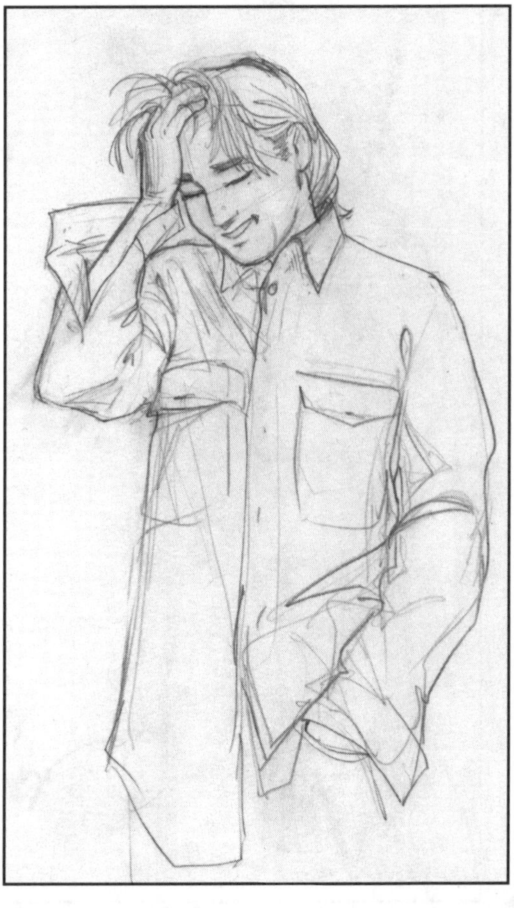

LEFT: David by Michelangelo
ABOVE: First cast drawing of SiP
RIGHT: David from sketchbook

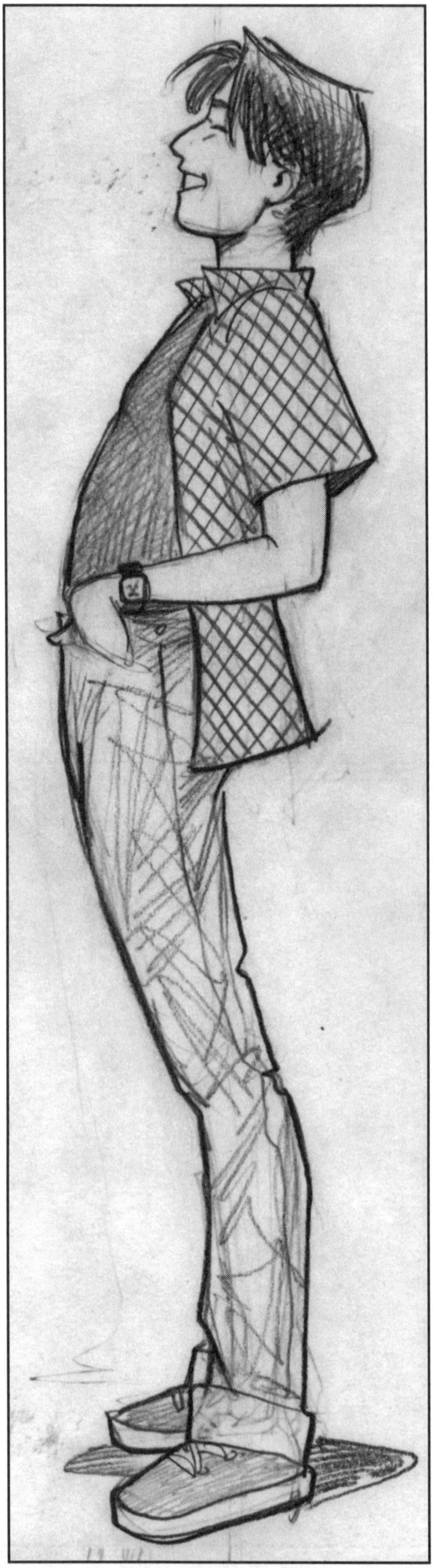
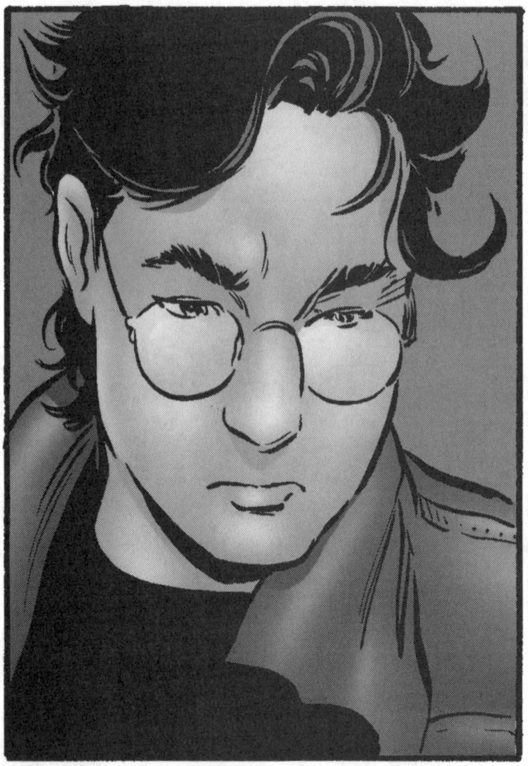
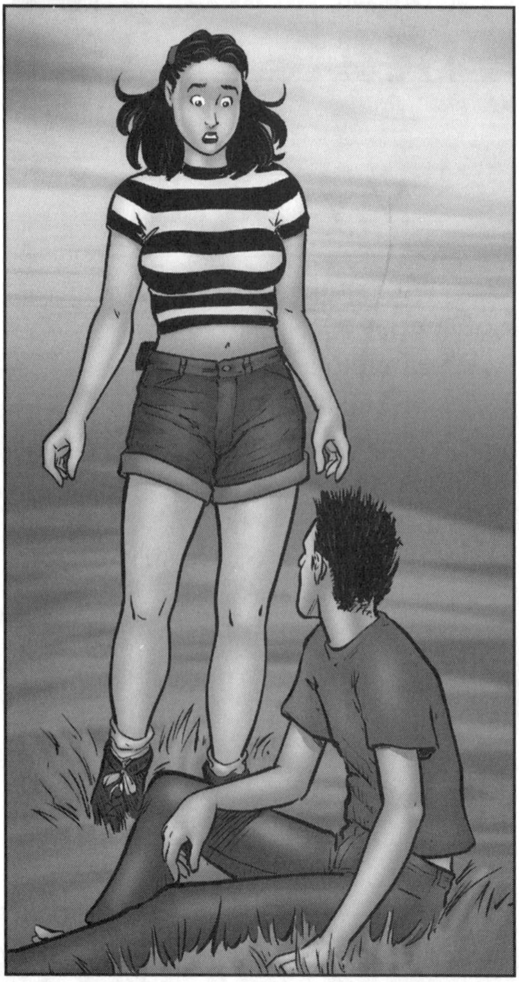

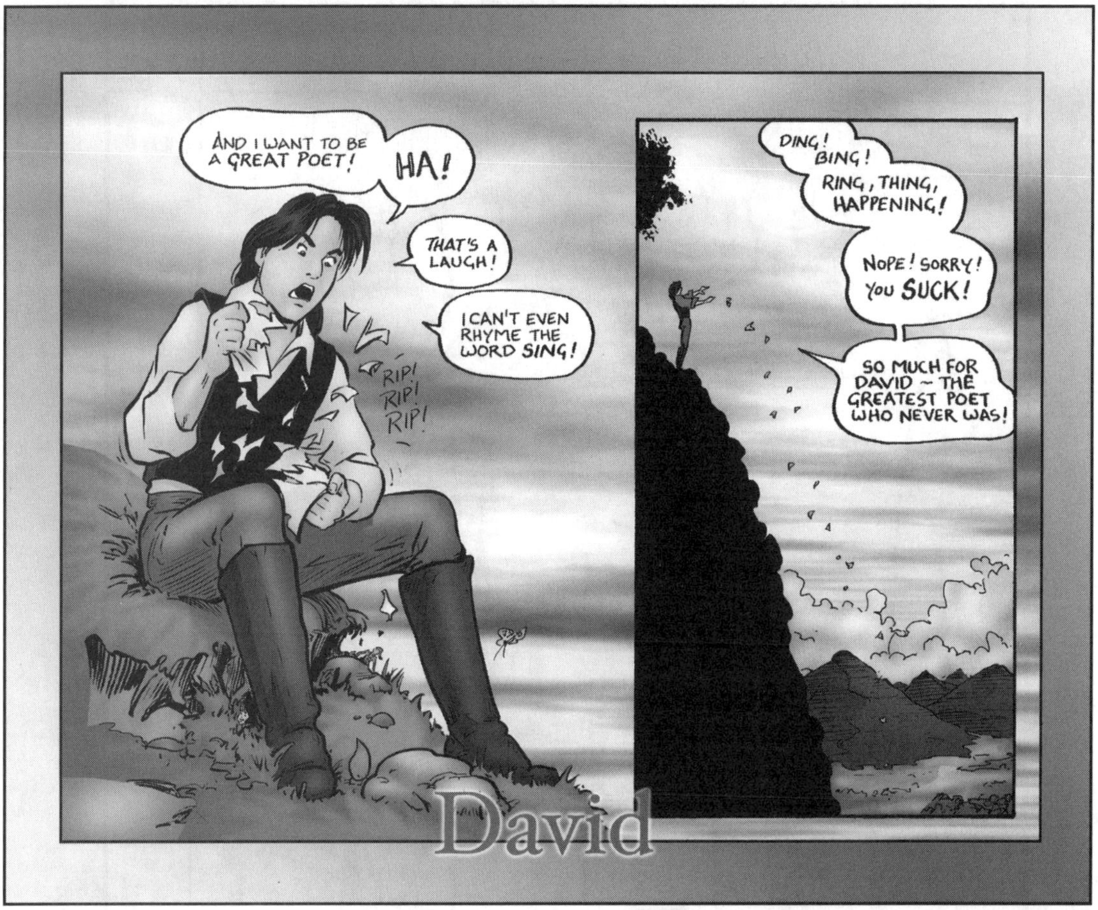
AND I WANT TO BE A GREAT POET!
HA!
THAT'S A LAUGH!
I CAN'T EVEN RHYME THE WORD SING!
RIP! RIP! RIP!
DING! BING! RING, THING, HAPPENING!
NOPE! SORRY! YOU SUCK!
SO MUCH FOR DAVID ~ THE GREATEST POET WHO NEVER WAS!
David

ABOVE: David in Xena parody, *Princess Warrior*
LEFT: David from Katchoo's sketchbook

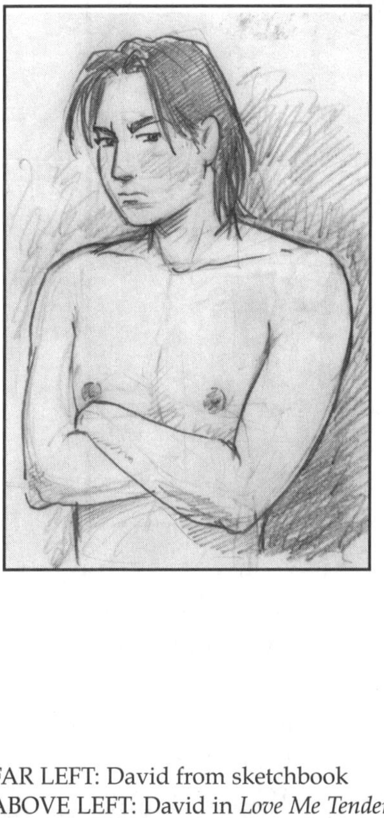

David is a creative person. When he makes his first appearance in issue #1 he is an art student and reads poetry to Katchoo from his sketchbook. He sleeps late, eats badly, reads a lot and couldn't care less about practical matters such as business, politics, the world economy or balanced checkbooks. He appreciates nature, philosophy, anything of beauty and a clean conscience.

SiP Fact

David is younger than Francine and Katchoo by several years. When we begin the SiP story in issue #1, the girls are in their mid-twenties; David is nineteen.

FAR LEFT: David from sketchbook
ABOVE LEFT: David in *Love Me Tender*
BOTTOM LEFT: David and Francine in *Child Of Rage*

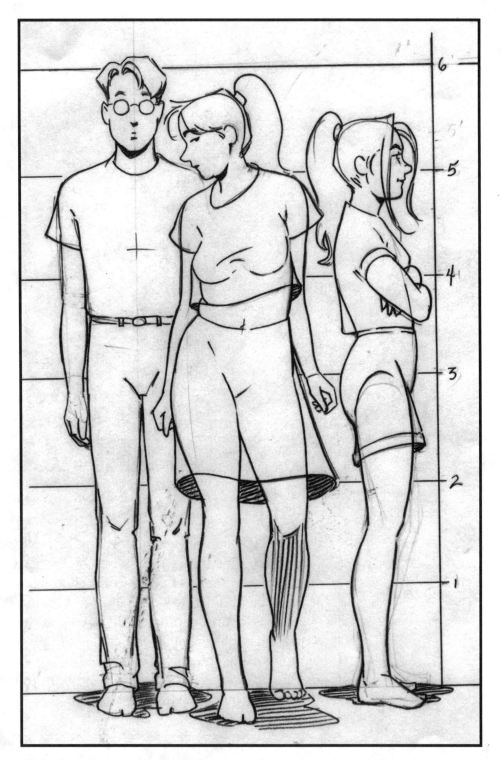

This drawing was originally done for an article in Wizard magazine about how to draw women, but it also shows the design of David with the SiP girls. Lucky guy. David is 5'11" tall...6' with hair.

Just after this picture was drawn, Francine's bump and grind got out of hand and David had to drag her back to the dressing room. We later discovered she'd eaten an entire box of Krispy Kreme donuts.

David poses with Katchoo and Francine in the Heart in Hand book.
David is wearing a Plato t-shirt, from the Paradise TOO comic strips.
Katchoo's cargo pants pocket contains a pack of Marlboro cigarettes and a
lighter. Nobody ever noticed that Francine's belt is made of handcuffs. Just
when you think she's conservative, she'll surprise you with something
like that. David and Katchoo have learned to roll with it.